PuzzleDuck Golf
Migrate to a More Efficient Game

Brad Clayton

Foreword by David Leadbetter

PuzzleDuck Golf by Brad Clayton is without doubt one of the most comprehensive game improvement books I have ever read. Brad does a phenomenal job of breaking down the various intricacies of the game into easy understandable concepts while taking a holistic approach to helping golfers improve. Brad's analogy of 'migrating to a better game' to that of a duck's migration is spot on! Once we understand what it is we need to do to in order to improve and have a picture and feel for it, it's all about staying the course and being consistent and committed in our effort as we strive to achieve our golfing goals!

In 2007 at the Carolinas Teaching Summit in Myrtle Beach I got to meet Brad personally and was struck by his enthusiasm for teaching the game and sharing his ideas with others. If I recall he received an award that day from the Carolinas PGA Section for his outstanding service in addition to his status as a PGA of America Master Teaching Professional accreditation in 2001. Brad demonstrates this same level of enthusiasm and passion to help golfers reach their potential in Puzzle Duck Golf as he outlines his four cornerstones for optimum performance: swing mechanics, mental clarity, physical ability, and equipment.

By taking a 'big picture' approach to helping players improve, PuzzleDuck Golf separates itself from many of the 'method' books which can pigeon hole players into thinking there is only one way to swing a golf club without taking into account the players talent level, physical build, or mindset. In addition, Brad does a great job of injecting his keen sense of humor for teaching and for life into his book, and as frustrating as this game can be at times a little fun and humor goes a long way.

I hope you enjoy PuzzleDuck Golf by Brad Clayton as much as I did. It's the next best thing to taking a lesson with Brad himself. Enjoy the read!

- David Leadbetter

PuzzleDuck Golf
Migrate to a More Efficient Game

By Brad Clayton

Copyright © 2019 by Brad Clayton. All rights reserved.

Printed in the United States of America.

Published by Brad Clayton, North Carolina, USA

Editor: Janet Burleson

Production Editor: Jennifer Stanley

Printing History:

December 2011 for First Edition, September 2019 Second Printing

Visit
PuzzleDuckGolf.com
to view the free training
videos illustrating the
lessons in this book.

Table of Contents

Who Is Brad Clayton?

My name is Brad Clayton. I am the EXTREMELY proud father of, in my eyes and heart, THE two most beautiful children and souls ever, Wallace "Nickolas" and "Winona" Juliana Clayton. They are without question the two best results of my life and the two best contributions to this world I have had to offer. I love you both. {O}

Fig. 1 – 1: Brad, Winona and Nickolas Clayton

Real, logical, stubborn, honest to a fault, faithful, loyal, loving, compassionate, committed, patient, respectful, passionate, resilient, and a touch of rebel are a few words I would use to describe myself. I work hard but, am not the best business man, as I tend to give my time away. I stand for what I believe in, even when that must be alone. The individual person defines class to me, not money or color. I take up for the underdawg, cry when someone hurts, and avoid confrontation, but never back down when pushed in a corner. I love my family, playing golf, riding horses, anything with my girl, and socializing. No, this is not a commercial:) just a piece of who I am. I read this to my mom and dad; they concurred; so I feel comfortable with this paragraph.

I have been playing golf since introduced to the game by my father Wallace Clayton when 7 years old in 1974. There was an immediate love. My mother Joyce would let me ride my bike to the club and could find me by looking for my dawg Lassie who was always following me around the course and close by. I was fortunate to grow up very close to a golf course, nine hole Thorndale Country Club; in a small town, Oxford, North Carolina; and in a time when parents had no fear of letting kids roam surrounding areas til dusk. Where did those times go?

I grew up playing outside exploring nature {have always been intrigued and drawn to the ways and values of Native Americans}, soccer, basketball, and of course golf. At the age of 12, I knew I was going to be a golf professional. Of course a touring professional was the first choice, but if not that, teaching would certainly be my career.
And, so it turned out….with very hard work on my game all my life, working odd jobs to live as I got older from selling boots, to lawn maintenance, to teaching bartending, to being an assistant golf professional, the help of my father {who has always had my back}, and a few other people here and there; I tried playing, but with limited success. I could go low and typically made lots of birdies, but also typically had a few shots here and there that were so loose big numbers followed. At age 20 I turned professional and my first round as a professional, shot 33 – 44 for

77. What a mixed bag. Signs of great stuff, then signs of, "what am I doing out here".

I continued to work very hard on my game and play, but never really understood clearly a few simple concepts that later would give me understanding and control of my golf ball. Had I understood then what I understand now, I feel very confident that I would have had a much more successful playing career that would have included the PGA Tour. But……..that is a BIG "if".

Since turning professional in 1987, I have played and primarily been a teaching professional full time, but worked as an assistant professional in Myrtle Beach, SC; Pinehurst, NC; and Linville, NC to become a PGA of America member from 1989 to 1992. After on and off playing mini tours and being an assistant professional from 1987 to 1994, I moved to Europe to teach and try the European tour. The teaching went ok and I did not make the tour full time, but it was well worth the experience and by far the greatest results of that time were my two children.

After opening The Golf Zone Practice and Learning Center in September of 1999 and three years of not really trying to compete, I privately considered playing again when I finally did truly understand what it took to control my golf ball, but a few other things at that time were my priority and happened, so I have remained focused on refining my teaching skills and spreading my love for the game through teaching and Instructional/Motivational/Trick Shot clinics. I GENUINELY care about each and every student I have ever worked with and take their results personally. It is my true desire and passion to help everyone I come in contact with to simplify and get the most out of their ability.

When I was twenty-something, my father encouraged me to go into insurance and take over his business making a very comfortable living. I told him that I would rather be happy, do what I love every day, and financially poor than monetarily wealthy, but doing something I did not love. I got my wish. :) I work hard almost every day and am monetarily poor {my intentions and efforts have ALWAYS been pure and for the good}, but I love what I do and feel like I have impacted many lives in a positive way. I am a very rich man in life in many ways with countless fantastic memories of family, friends, and career that money cannot buy. If I die today, I have had one hell of a ride that my mom {who I have always confided in and "shocked"} and others have encouraged me to write a book on as well. Who knows…..if there was ever any interest……maybe?

Through the great game of golf, I am and have been very fortunate to have traveled, worked, and competed with MANY an interesting character, throughout the United States, Europe, and once in Canada. I moved about every six months to a new location for about 12 years and traveled as well. It has been a blessing to see so many beautiful places, meet so many wonderful people, and experience so many different cultures. As most journeyman golf professionals have, there are many stories that go along with those adventures.

Through all of those travels and adventures there are many times that stand out and bring a smile and warm feeling, but there are four events that stand out in my life that truly humble me yet at the same moment make me prouder than words can express. Two of those were the births of my children, Nickolas and Winona, and the other two were Professional; when named Carolinas PGA Teacher of the Year in 2008 and when I earned my Master Professional status. Unbelievable raw emotion each event burned in my soul.
I am not exactly your typical PGA Professional, let alone PGA Master Professional. I tend to ride a little off the beaten trail. Those that know me are saying, "that is forrrrrr sure". For those that do not, some have said, "Did they write the movie Tin Cup about you?" There are many parallels and much to add.

If you take lessons from me, you may on first sight say, "who is this long haired, one handed guy?" {I lost my right hand on May 18, 2000 completing The Golf Zone in Oxford, North Carolina} and "can this guy really teach?" It has become my experience that most people only care that you care and can make them better. That I truly care is undeniable and I am very proud of the results my students get.

When teaching a new student I am always dressed professionally, but once a relationship is formed, on a few occasions, have been known to teach in short pants, barefooted, or in flip flops in the summer or boots and jeans in the winter (I can feel some of my colleagues cringing now. You may even catch me giving a checkup lesson or helping a range patron from the back of my daughters' horse, Gypsy.

Fig. 1 - 2

Gypsy also grazes on the range at times and might just walk into the teaching bay and say hello or stand and watch. Not something you see every day {Fig. 1 – 3}. My children's dawg Bridgette is often laying around watching me teach and practice. That's her spot {Fig. 1 - 4}.

Fig. 1 – 3   Fig. 1 – 4

I am probably not always the clean cut professional the PGA of America would like to project when not teaching and on that occasion mentioned when I am. I am just relaxed that way and prefer to be in jeans, boots or flop flips, don't clean cut shave, and usually wear my hair a little longer than the norm, but also enjoy dressing nicely and always dress the role when necessary. It's just who I am, but I feel like I have represented the PGA of America positively throughout my career and try to make a "difference" in many ways both unconventionally and conventionally {Fig. 1 – 5 and 6}.

Fig. 1 – 5   Fig. 1 – 6

All that being said; I am TRULY proud to be a PGA of America member and feel as though our logo and organization are part of my identity. {Fig. 1 – 7}

Fig. 1 – 7

Losing my hand in May of 2000 has truly been a blessing for me. It has given me the opportunity to stand out a little, test myself, relate to others, and I think more importantly, be related to by others. By dealing in a positive way with what some people consider a life changing accident, I

may be able to touch a few more lives than I ever would have been able to with two hands and arms.

Patience, perseverance, and a positive outlook are a few qualities I have been very fortunate to be blessed with. I must say I have NEVER waivered from being positive in any part of my life through much adversity. For me it truly is what it is; embrace it, experience it, and move forward in a way that motivates and spreads positive energy to all you encounter. Experience each event, express true and pure emotion, then move on. Everyone has their own stories in their own relative way, it is simply how we choose to react to all that life throws our way that gives us an opportunity to make a difference and spread that positive energy.

I thoroughly enjoy doing my clinique that is full of practical instruction, motivation, and trick shots all beat up together with a laugh or thirteen, and hope very much to be doing more in the near future; ESPECIALLY for our Wounded Warriors, that have their own challenges to overcome when returning home from battle injured and/or with a different outlook on life. THANK YOU to them ALL!

Fig. 1 - 8   Fig. 1 – 9

So............ I will continue to teach and play the game that has shaped my life and what I have truly loved and had a passion for since the age of 7 years. I will continue to teach and play THE greatest past time and game in so many ways until it is my time to be gone from here. It is my sincerest hope that the efforts of this book help ALL that read it in some if not many ways and in some way helps me leave at least a few thoughts of me when my time does come. That day will be one more large time. I will wish I was there. :)

There have been many people that have influenced my career in one way or another; some by support, some with golf knowledge and opinions, some by providing a place to teach, some by giving me a chance to participate, and some in ways that are not describable. Each person or entity knows his role. In order of appearance or at least close, I would like to say thank you!

My Family, I love and appreciate you all:

- My mom, Joyce Lawhon
- My Dad, Wallace Clayton
- My Children, Wallace "Nickolas" Clayton and "Winona" Juliana Clayton
- My Sister, Franchelle Stevens
- My moms' Husband Buck Lawhon
- My Dads friend Pat Oakley
- All of my dawgs, especially Brittany and Bridgette….and my daughters horse Gypsy….they are/were always happy to see me and very good listeners. :)

Others:

- Wimpy Caldwell
- Jimmy Powell

- Bill Lytton
- Ronnie Reitz
- Ed Ibarguen
- David Leadbetter
- Jim Fellner
- Doug Thompson
- Willis Denmark
- Bill Dicus
- The PGA of America and The Carolinas Section
- Dick Tiddy
- Every student I have ever worked with
- Bill Strausbaugh
- Al Nelson
- Manfred Muckenauer
- Volker Knornsheld
- Dr. Marshall Redding
- Dan Brooks
- Ben Hynson
- Rich Parker
- Ron Schmid
- The Granville County Emergency Squad
- Dr. Scott Levin / Duke University Staff / The Hyperbaric Chamber and staff
- Ronnie Morgan and his Staff
- Don and Janet Burleson
- Sonny Belcher
- Neal Senter

- Mike Harmon
- Joe Matheny
- Jimmy Hamilton
- Chad Kufen
- Bob Byrnes
- Mike Woodall
- ALL of the brave men and women of OUR Armed Forces and their families that have sacrificed so much for our Country. It is an unbelievable honor to work with our Wounded Warriors that return from the battlefield different than when they went and hopefully make a positive difference in their new lives. Thank you to those that were not injured, those that were, those that lost their human life, and all of their families.

A Special THANK YOU to David Leadbetter for taking his time to write such a kind Forward for this book. He is the one that we "Teaching" Professionals need to thank for his pioneering efforts to make "Teaching" the game of golf a full time career rather than a past time for a Club Professional! Thank you also to Sean Hogan for his role in getting the Forward done.

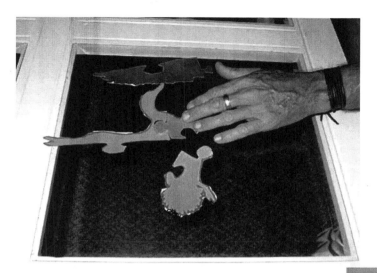

What the Heck is PuzzleDuck Golf?

The title and sub-title of this book as well as the original title, that I did not use, have evolved from some of my beliefs and sayings after many years of playing and teaching the great game of golf. Try using the explanation of the title and the analogies and thoughts below to help you understand and get through the sometimes, painful and arduous journey to becoming a better player.

The "Puzzle" in "PuzzleDuck" comes from comparing the process of building a golf swing and game with putting together a jigsaw puzzle {Fig. 2 - 1}.

Fig. 2 – 1

A golf swing can be related to a puzzle in that it is hard to know what the completed puzzle or swing looks like until all of the pieces have been put together. With a puzzle, you fit a few pieces together, but certainly cannot make out the picture (of course you know what the picture is, you looked at the box cover :). Then a few more fit and then a few more, but still there is no full picture. Then you fit a few more and then some more and finally, through a significant amount of patience and perseverance you start to see some shapes and forms resembling the box cover. And so is a golf swing and the game as a whole, you make an adjustment, but the adjustment doesn't fit with your previous swing and its' compensations, so your shots change. They may be better, normally they are not worse, but they are different, and that can be unsettling. So you work on those adjustments, all the while cursing me for what's happening, but we can't see the results yet because we haven't completed the puzzle.

I do not have a magic potion. When you come back after a week of practice and have significantly improved the adjustment/s from the previous hour, we put another piece to the puzzle in. As we continue to put the pieces together so do the results begin to improve and we start to see a clearer picture – better results. Please, do not perceive this to mean that there are individual parts of a swing. A golf swing is a continuous flowing motion. Adjustments in positions, directions, sequences, and angles can be worked on individually, but eventually must be blended together to form a flowing motion. As you put more and more pieces of the swing puzzle together, you become a more efficient ball striker. No one ever has and no one ever will always get all of the pieces to fit every time, {we are human beings}, but the more pieces that do, the more consistently you will see the picture and the more efficient and consistent your ball striking will be.

Not only does the puzzle apply to your golf swing, but to the game as a whole. Building and improving a "golf game" has many pieces that make the whole; bunker shots, chipping, pitching, putting, driving the ball, irons, recovery shots, course management, emotion management, physical limitations and fitness, equipment, and more. The PuzzleDuck logo has four pieces to the Duck {Fig. 2 – 2}. These four pieces represent the four components that, to me, make up peak performance: swing mechanics, attitude and course management, physical limitations and fitness, and equipment. The four parts make up the whole, and if there is a weakness in any part, the whole will be affected. So, the better each "piece" is, the more consistent and complete the player.

The Four Pieces also represent the four main areas I focus on in any golf swing. The Full Swing Chapter will elaborate on these four areas.

Fig. 2 – 2

Golf swing and game improvement is a process; one that takes time, patience, and perseverance, which is where the "Duck" in "PuzzleDuck" comes from. I like to express this process and compare a students' progress to that of a duck. I love to see a student and suddenly hear a quacking noise jokingly come from them as they pick fun of their migration. Ducks migrate, as do we making swing adjustments. The flaw or flaws in your swing are seldom, if ever going to change to perfection in one swing or over night, but we are trying to migrate to perfection. We, as humans will never reach perfection and some will get closer than others, but the closer we get to perfection, the better the results. I like to compare the ducks migration to that of a student in transition/migration. Ducks start in the north {in the fall} and fly south. Their trek is long and full of hard work and frustration, but they keep flapping their wings, trying to get closer to their goal, their destination. They persevere through wind, rain, cold, heat, and any other element Mother Nature can throw at them, but they keep flapping their wings, getting closer and closer to their goal {Fig. 2 – 3}. If they could, I chance a guess that they would choose the magic of a Wizards'/Witches' potion to make their trip over in a flash, but that does not exist, so they keep flapping.

Fig. 2 – 3

Compare the ducks migration to you and your improvement. Every practice swing or drill done correctly with a purpose to improve your swing is like each flap of the wings trying to get closer to a destination {Fig. 2 – 4}. After each drill or practice swing done correctly, with a purpose, and focused you are getting closer to your goal of improving your swing. It may not change instantly, but you are migrating toward a better strike. The more you practice properly, the closer you will get to the correct position or motion and the better you will perform. Understand that neither you nor anyone else will ever get to perfection every time, but the closer and more consistently you get to it the better and more consistent your golf shots will be. Migrate.

Fig. 2 – 4

The original title to this book was going to be "There Is No Magic Potion, But Golf Just Doesn't Have To Be That Hard", which is a true belief of mine. "There Is No Magic Potion" comes from the many times I have used the words, "I do not have a magic potion that will make you your best immediately for a lasting period of time". If I did, I would be teaching golf for free on my own tropical island and everyone would be breaking par. Sure, I can give a "tip" lesson as can anyone, but that will not give you the consistency and understanding I like to instill in every student. What I do provide is reality, understanding, direction, enthusiasm, and hope for those prepared to improve over time. This, I guarantee; assuming a reasonable amount of consistent effort is given by the student.

My golf lesson for a full golf swing, lasts a minimum of four hours, one hour taken once a week for four weeks {I do offer longer programs to include all aspects of golf, but four is the minimum for a full swing}. This gives us both a realistic opportunity to implement lasting adjustments. I make it clear to each student in the beginning that I do not have that "magic potion", but need time to make adjustments that are effective and last. I have seen the results of and heard too many stories from students that blame their demise and/or lack of improvement on "a" lesson they took from a Golf Professional. I try to explain that it may or may not have been the best lesson ever given, but it could have simply been that there was not enough time for the professional to make all of the adjustments necessary to achieve consistency.

There is but so much that can be done in one hour before any student is overwhelmed and paralyzed with information, only to become frustrated; losing confidence in their ability as well as the professionals'. In the beginning stages of working with a student, rarely have I seen one hour be enough time to teach the swing to a point that the student truly understands and strikes consistent golf shots to the best of their ability. Sure, there are those that really only want to get a tip here or there that will help them get through the day without too much embarrassment, but for anyone who is truly trying to get better, one hour, simply will not do.

After a solid beginning of at least four sessions and there is a solid base of understanding, a single lesson from time to time is an effective check up to make sure the student is remaining "on track". This is not to say that four is the magic number, but a very solid beginning. I feel very confident that in four weeks I can help anyone feel better, improve, and understand more about their golf swing; but rarely in one hour.

One more time, there is no magic potion. Great golf doesn't come overnight or without constructive effort, but over time and with purposeful practice. One more analogy I like to use is to think of your game as a snow ball. The snowball/knowledge starts small, but as you roll/learn along the snowball and you pick up more and more snow/knowledge. The snowball gets bigger and bigger as does your repertoire of shots and understanding of how to strike the ball more consistently and under control. This analogy does not only apply to striking a golf ball, but playing the game as a whole. There is so much to learn about playing the game that no one ever has known or ever will know it all, but the longer you play and the better student you are, the more knowledge you will pick up and the bigger your "snowball" will become.

The second part of the original title "But Golf Just Doesn't Have To Be That Hard" comes from seeing people, amateurs and professionals alike, make the game of golf so complicated and confusing that it can be maddening. Don't get me wrong, I'm not saying that golf is easy to master, but I am saying it can be easy to enjoy and that people in general tend to over complicate the game, anything really, as a whole. As far as I am concerned, making a consistent effective golf swing is slightly harder than easy {figure that one out}. But it is true; the game does not have to be made {as my friend John Maginnes would say} "harder than Chinese arithmetic".

People tend to struggle because they are not clear about what to do, over analyze and try to do too much at one time, do not have consistent positive direction, and have anxiety about change. It can be a never ending spiral of futility. There is so much going on in a swing, yet so little. It can be made as complicated as you like or as simple as you like. I choose to be as simple as I can be, with my students, as well as myself and will convey that theme throughout this book.

I can go just as deep about the potential complex motions of golf swings as the next guy, but do not feel that to be necessary, nor effective in teaching or trying to learn a swing or the game as a whole. In fact, the older I get, the less confusion I see going on in the technique of a swing, short or long, and the clearer the simplicity of the overall motion becomes. It's not that hard! Striking a golf ball solid, straight, and consistent really can be made, flat out, "slightly harder than easy", if you have the correct attitude, understand some simple technique concepts, and are patiently impatient {patient with the process, but not complacent}.

We must all remember that golf is a game of non perfections. No one hits the perfect shot every time! It is all about managing the emotions and imperfections of being a human and minimizing the amount of error in your worst golf shots. Playing the game as a whole is no different. Remember, simplify, be a duck, put the puzzle together, and let your snowball grow. Build a solid foundation and always migrate closer and closer to a more efficient swing and game with direction, adding to what you know and do. You will improve, it's really not that hard!

How to Get the Most Out of This Book or Any Golf Instruction

The information in this book is simply what I teach on a daily basis. I make no claim that it is the only way to play the game. It is merely the way that I teach and play after many years of experience, my own trial and error, study, lessons both taken and given, and when you get right down to it; just plain common sense.
I do not follow any one persons' theories or thought process, but have been influenced by many people throughout my career and life.

I have used my experiences and bits and pieces from many to form what is my approach to this fascinating game called golf. I must say that I formed and validated most of my opinions through my own experiences of trial and error, using information learned and trying to "figure it out"; or as Lee Trevino has said "digging it out of the dirt". My conclusion is, there is no magic potion and it takes a little time, but once I understood some simple concepts, it really wasn't as hard as I had made it and it doesn't have to be that way for you either.

The instruction in this book is written to explain what "I" feel you should be doing, not telling you what you should not be doing. There are simply too many variables to consider all of the possibilities and combinations of positions and motions, especially when talking about full swings. It is also written as if talking to a right handed player for simplicity. If you are left handed player, simply flip the lefts to right and the rights to left.

There is always room to be an individual, on either side of the guidelines that I present throughout this book, assuming the appropriate compensations are made, but in my opinion, the closer you get to the suggestions made, the better you will be. However, remember that there is no substitute for good old fashioned, hands on instruction, where a qualified teacher can see you and the many things that make your golf swing unique.

That being said, here are a few things to help you get the most out of your experience reading this book, watching a DVD, or hands on instruction.

First and foremost, there is little hope for success if you do not have the correct attitude. With a positive attitude; you must be open to change and prepared to give change a chance to develop. If you hit shots that are less than desirable, try to look at those results in an objective manner. That shot was what it was for a reason. You must stay with the process, with a positive attitude, and learn from it. That is easy for me to say, I am not the one going through what you may be going through; but I have.

It is very hard to remain positive when you feel different and are getting new results, especially if those results are less than desirable, but you must push through. Learning is very difficult if you are putting out negative energy. So, in case I haven't said it enough, I can not over express the importance of being positive through your "migrating" period :).

Second, you must trust the instructor/author you are listening to and be committed to making the adjustments recommended. Remember, the reason you began to read this book or take lessons is because you wanted to learn more and/or were not satisfied with your game. The only way to get more positive results is to make sound adjustments. You chose the author/instructor for a reason, so you must trust and commit to his/her judgment. Obviously, after a reasonable period of time, you should evaluate how you feel about your progress and what you are doing. At that time you can decide to continue or cut the line, but until ample opportunity has been given to the process, you must trust and commit.

Third, try and grade "yourself" and not so much what the ball does. Especially in the beginning, your swing adjustments will probably not match your old swing, so try to grade your success on how well you make the swing adjustment and not so much on what the ball does. Once again, I know that is easy for me to say, I am not the one potentially hitting sideways shots, but I feel strongly about the importance of thinking this way.

As you stay with what you are doing and learning, your shots will get better the more pieces of the puzzle you put together, but you must improve the adjustment at hand before moving on, regardless of what the ball does at that time. It makes no sense to go on to another piece of the puzzle if you have not sufficiently mastered the adjustment you have been working on. So make the adjustment; get it done; the faster you overcome the flaw the faster you can progress and learn something new.

One of my favorite quotes is by a man named Verne Hill {I have no idea who he is/was}, "If you always do what you always did, you'll always get what you always got". So; to get different results you must change, but you must be committed to those changes and stick with them. If you give up on them because you do not see immediate positive golf shots, you will get sucked into a spiral of indecision, causing only more confusion and inconsistent results. "Stay the course" and grade yourself, not the ball, even if things initially look less than desirable. Give it a little time.

Fourth, be patiently impatient with the process. Give the process time and a chance to work, but without being complacent. Be patient and understand that the process of improvement takes time, but impatient with the desire and drive necessary to push yourself to improve; today. You want it now.

It is much like working out. You can go to the gym for two hours and work out hard, but at the end of the day you will not be able to see the fruits of your labor, only that you can feel pain. Over the next week, your desire to change your appearance and the way you feel drives you to continue the work out each day, but still no visible results other than the soreness beginning to subside. However, over time with consistent productive workouts you start to see the difference in your body and the way you feel. The results of your efforts begin to become noticeable, as it will be in your golf game. It takes positive consistent practice, being patiently impatient, and time.

Fifth, understanding, in clarity, what you are trying to do is crucial. It is a must to significant improvement. If you do not understand what to tell your body to do, obviously, you will have little success getting it done and will send mixed and incomplete signals to your body. Take your time reading and visualize what the words are saying. The illustrations and video will help you with your visualization, but you must clearly understand your objective. Ask your instructor whatever questions necessary to get ANY question marks out of your head. If you have questions about this book......email them to me through the puzzleduckgolf.org website.

Once you have the correct mental picture and are clear about your objectives, you can literally change in an instant. Your body will do what you tell it to do, relative to your limitations. Try it now. Within reason, tell a part of your body to do something {rotate or lift your arm}. I am willing to bet that it did what it was told. You don't know how, you just told yourself to do it, and it did. Making adjustments to your golf swing is no different, if you are committed to the command. Tell your body to do something and it will. You need only understand and trust what you are trying to do and then simply do it, but, and this is paramount, in the beginning, with no regard for what the golf ball does or how the adjustment feels.

Contrary to what you may have heard, there is no such animal as "muscle memory". Muscles do not think and cannot remember, they only do what they are told to do by your brain, so you must clearly understand your objective. Maybe that's why a person in a comma does nothing or why you missed getting off an exit ramp because you were distracted by ... a conversation. There are many examples to disprove the statement of "muscle memory".

It is your subconscious mind that allows you to multi task, but only after your conscious mind has understood and processed the command to your muscles enough to be committed to your subconscious. My point is; you can change in an instant; you need only understand, commit, and tell yourself what to do with no apprehensions.

Sixth, you can spend large sums of money on the best books, DVDs, best teachers, mental coaches, and trainers, but their effectiveness is limited to the effort and quality of practice implemented by you on a consistent basis. This does not mean you must hit balls and train 10 hours a day like a touring professional, but you do need to put forth some committed and consistent effort. It will not happen just because you "want it to". Once again, there is no magic potion.

Seventh, I like to look at a players' level of play as being on layers in a pyramid. My Model Player is on the peak of the pyramid. There will never be anyone that will join my Model Player on the top, because we are all humans and there is not nor will there ever be a human that can make a perfect swing, every time.
Everyone starts on the bottom layer, which is the largest layer. Most will stay there, because they have little solid direction and lack the desire or patience to learn, but some will get better and get to the next level. Most of those will stay there, but some will move up, and so on until there are very few that are on the upper levels, as is represented by the narrowing of the pyramid the higher up one goes. Physical limitations, mental limitations, and desire will determine how high up the pyramid one can go, but every person has their personal best relative to those limitations and desire.

How far up the pyramid you make it depends on many combinations of many factors and outside of a severe physical limitation, the most important being; desire. Just how far are you prepared to go in training three of the four areas that I think make up peak performance – swing mechanics {technique}, physical abilities and limitations, mental game {attitude and course management}.

The last piece, equipment that is correctly fit to you is important and relatively easy this day and age, but you should know that you cannot buy a game through a set of golf clubs. Sure, you can get top of the line clubs fit to you and they may help to a degree, but there is a limit. You still must know how to use the clubs effectively. They will not swing on their own. It is like me having state of the art brain surgery instruments. I could do a surgery, but I don't think you would like me doing one on you, because I have no clue what to do with them and they are not likely to perform on their own, no matter how state of the art they are.

Getting clubs that are draw or fade biased to compensate for swing flaws makes little sense to me either. Unless you have a physical limitation that needs help, get golf clubs fit to your specs with no compensations and learn how to swing them with an effective technique, so you can reach your full potential.

Once again, the equipment part is relatively easy. That leaves us with the three areas that desire will greatly influence. These three are greatly interrelated, for each area significantly affects the efficiency of the other two.

You can have a great understanding of swing mechanics, but if you are not physically capable of making those swings, you have two choices if the limitations are changeable: 1} do something about them by working out, stretching, and over all getting physically fit or 2} accept the fact that your improvement will be limited to the range of motion and strength your body has.

If your physical limitations can not be improved, you must accept the limitation for what it is, improvise, and get real good in other areas of your game that that limitation does not affect so dramatically. A common example might be, if you lack distance, I strongly suggest you get really good with your short game.

Athleticism and talent are great plusses, but mean little if your mechanics are not solid. In return, great mechanics and ball striking mean little if you can not manage yourself or your ball. One can have athleticism and mechanics, but with the wrong attitude can go but so far. You can think positive and "want" to all you want, but if your mechanics aren't solid, it will not work.

So it is, as in many things, the parts become the whole. Full potential can only be reached when you have all of the ingredients; kind of like your moms' recipe for your favorite dish. If you leave something out or put in too much or too little of something, it's just not the same.

To get to the top layers of the pyramid, you must have all of the pieces and how complete you are with each will greatly influence how far up you go. This book will address and give direction for mechanics and personal management. I suggest you see a professional trainer in your area for physical fitness and a qualified club fitter for your clubs.

Summary
I think that most anyone can learn to play golf, even those that are not physically gifted or have physical issues, whether they are visible or not. I have seen people play and enjoy golf that are just flat out amazing. If a positive attitude is there, the heart and desire to excel is there, and the willingness to learn is there, it can be done. It may come a little harder and require more work for some than others, but with a positive attitude, good direction, perseverance, and a will to learn and succeed, much can be overcome and you can and will move up the pyramid.

Commitment and Pre Shot Routine

The significance of a pre shot routine is all too often over looked. Whether it is from lack of discipline or lack of knowledge about its' value, too few people incorporate this all important part of any golf shot. Why do the best players (most successful athletes, period) in the world have a routine that they use? **It works!** But, why does it work and what does it help? Time and time again at the champions interview you hear players explain how he/she relied on his/her pre shot routine to focus on the process of executing the shot, rather than on the surroundings, outcome, or the pressures of the moment. The result is a product of the process, so when the process is good the chances for positive results are greatly increased.

Concentrating for the duration of a round is extremely difficult, if not impossible, let alone boring, draining, and miserable. Therefore, a routine helps you concentrate in small focused bursts that are manageable. Also, if you lose your focus by distraction or negative thoughts at any time during your routine you have a place to go to and start over.

A routine helps you stay focused and committed to the shot, and assuming you have solid swing mechanics, in my opinion, being focused and committed are the two most critical components of consistent successful golf shots. Whether you have made the correct decision or not, you must be focused and committed to that decision and execute.

So, what is a pre shot routine? A pre shot routine is a series of events that an athlete performs leading up to the actual action of hitting a golf ball, shooting a free throw, preparing to bat, or serve in tennis to name a few. The next few paragraphs will explain the components of what I teach and think is a sound and productive pre-shot routine for **every shot** you hit

with the exception of tap in putts. It also happens to be my thought process and pre-shot routine, but can be used by you as a guideline. Modify these ideas to find what works best for you or use it as is.

First and foremost, once you have evaluated your situation, you must commit to the golf shot and club chosen, right or wrong {Fig. 4 – 1}.

I AM going to hit this 6 iron with a 5 yard draw to my target.

If you have been playing golf for any length of time you can certainly recall many times that you were indecisive over the ball, but continued and hit the shot anyway. I am willing to bet that the outcomes of those shots were not favorable, many more times than they were. Among many scenarios, you may have been between clubs, had the driver in your hands on a tight hole, the wind could have been gusting making you second guess the club chosen, or you could have been unsure of the line or speed of a putt, but you simply were not clearly committed and continued with only hopes of success and no conviction.

How many times after those shots did you say, "I knew that was wrong" or "why didn't I stop?". The mistake was not necessarily that you chose the wrong club, shot, or line; but, more often than not, the half hearted swing or over swing you made trying to back off or force it to work, even though inside you knew you were not sure and committed. It is better to hit the wrong club or shot with commitment than a half hearted swing.

Focusing and committing to each shot is no walk in the park. There is a certain amount of discipline required to achieve focus and commitment, each shot throughout a round. Few; professionals included, are able to do so, but the better you get, the positives are overwhelming when right or wrong you evaluate, decide, commit, and then execute. When it is all said and done, analyze the outcome, and then move on. If it was not the greatest shot, fine, but you know you did your best and gave the shot the best possible chance for success by focusing and committing to your decisions.

Once the lie of the ball and the situation has been evaluated and the shot and club selection has been committed to, I think you will find that most, if not all, successful pre shot routines begin from behind the ball on the target line {a line from behind the ball through the ball to the target or if there is curve in the shot on that curve line} and about three paces in distance. This will put you in position to see the target relative to your ball and visualize the shot you are preparing to play. The three paces back is a good distance to see the complete picture yet a short enough distance to cut down on time for distractions both internally and externally.

Visualizing the swing and results you wish to produce is of great value. Clearly seeing the swing and outcome you desire requires practice, but the better you become at it the better your results will be. As you look at your target, see in your mind how you would like your ball to arrive there {what shape and trajectory will it take?}.

Then, visualize the swing necessary to produce those results. Even if you are not an accomplished enough player to actually hit the shot or make the swing you are visualizing, it is still beneficial. Use your favorite tour player as a model if that helps. Once you have a clear picture in your mind, rehearse that swing as your practice swing.

I suggest rehearsing the swing {practice swing} **before** you get into your pre shot routine rather than after. This means from your drive to your putt, that you go straight in, aim the face, set up, then play your shot rather than taking a practice swing beside the ball, then playing. By the way, if you make a practice swing behind your ball, be sure not to take a divot in the direction of your ball and move it or cover it with turf. This whole process may read like a lot of time and effort, but it actually takes place in only moments.

Now that you have evaluated your lie and shot required, committed to your decisions, visualized what you would like to do, rehearsed the motion, and gotten into your starting position {behind the ball}, it is now time to actually begin your routine and execute. I think every pre-shot routine should begin with a trigger. A "trigger" is the act you perform to start your pre shot routine. There are many ways to trigger the start of your routine, from taking a deep breath (my trigger), to tugging on your shirt, to tightening your glove, to tapping your club on the ground, or any small action that signifies your beginning.

This "trigger" gives you a starting point. The completion of your swing in balance will give you an ending point. The time between the trigger and the end of the swing should last no more than about twenty five seconds and as far as I am concerned, within reason, the shorter the better. Mine lasts from fifteen to twenty seconds and when I am really on it narrows to eighteen consistently. Try not to get too caught up in being perfectly exact with your time, but you would like to be consistent. The longer you take, the more time negative thoughts and distractions have to derail your focus and commitment. This does not mean to rush, but go about your routine with a purpose and no wasted time or energy.

There are many routines and triggers that are used throughout the golf world. No one way is necessarily the best. You should comprise one that makes you feel comfortable and helps you stay focused and committed to the task at hand. The following is my model after the shot has been evaluated and totally committed to:

1} Stand behind the ball on the line you have committed to start it on, approximately three steps away {Fig. 4 – 2}.

Taking a deep breath and visualizing shot

Fig. 4 – 2

If you are going to shape your ball, this means on the starting line the amount left or right you intend to bend the ball. If it is a putt that breaks, this means on the line the ball must start on to allow for enough break.

2} Use a slow **deep** breathe as your trigger to get oxygen in your body and set yourself at ease. You may also want to add a roll of your neck and shoulders to help relieve any extra tension.

3} Approach the ball holding the club in one of three ways: In your left hand, in your right hand, or in both with your grip in tact. Experiment with all three and use the one that feels most comfortable to you {Fig. 4 - 3}.

Fig. 4 – 3

Approaching the ball with club in "both" hands :) HA.

4} If, North is above the ball, as you are looking at the ball in your address position, South is behind you, West to your left and East to your right, try and approach the ball from the South/East Quadrant with your right foot in approximately its' correct position and your left foot very close to your right and swiveled slightly open. Always work your way toward the target {Fig. 4 – 4}.

Aiming club face first

{Fig. 4 – 4}

5} **Aim the clubface first** and then set your body to the clubface {assuming you are going to hit a straight shot, a line across your feet, legs, hips, shoulders, arms, and eye line should be perpendicular to a square club face}. I, personally, do not use an intermediate target to help me line up {a point just in front of your ball in line with your target line}, but you should try one. If it helps you aim, use one; if not, do not. Once you are lined up your attention should now return to the target itself. In the words of the great Harvey Penick, "take dead aim" or Mel Gibson in The Patriot telling his kids to "aim small miss small" {Fig. 4 – 4}.

6} Stay in motion with some subtle movement in your feet, shoulders, arms, and wrists. This motion is called a "waggle". It helps stave off tension and creates a rhythm for your swing. Your waggle should and normally will match the rhythm and tempo of your swing, so be smooth and rhythmical, relative to your tempo. The slower the better for me.

7} When your intuition tells you it is time to go, then go {this should be a consistent time}. If you feel like you are over the ball too long, can not get committed, have negative thoughts, or are distracted; **start over.**

8} Your swing is complete when you are standing in balance and facing your target. {Fig. 4 – 5}

Finished in balance with back foot vertical and facing my target

{Fig. 4 – 5}

Once again, this process may read like it is very involved and time consuming, but it really is not. A routine will help you organize and focus your thoughts and process to help each action be done with a purpose. The entire process of evaluating the lie, choosing the golf shot, choosing the club, and executing the golf shot, should rarely take more than a minute. Be decisive with your choices, commit, focus, and execute. Your first instincts are the purest and typically, not always, but typically the ones to go with. The seconds, thirds, fourths, and so on are all second guesses. The more time you spend analyzing the more confusion has a chance to set in. I am not trying to say to be hap hazard about evaluating the shot and executing it, but be expeditious and go about it concisely and with a purpose.

Your pre shot routine leading up to the moment of swinging your club, should have helped you remain committed to the golf shot you are attempting. You must now trust what you have committed to and swing; right or wrong. When the swing is over, all you can do is evaluate the outcome and learn from it. There is no need to be angry if the result is poor or overly excited if the result is favorable. Hopefully, you did your best and gave yourself the best possible chance to succeed. Analyze the outcome, good or bad and be done with it. Now enjoy the down time of being outside alone, with friends, competitors, and always with nature {Fig.4 - 6, and Fig.4 -7}.

Fig. 4 – 6   Fig. 4 – 7

Then go do it again. On average, you will spend approximately four hours in a round of eighteen holes. If you shoot ninety {a random score chosen}, and for each shot you take one minute for the total process of evaluating and choosing the shot, choosing the club, and going through your routine, you will have one and a half hours actually invested in "playing" the game. The rest of the time, two and a half hours, is getting around the course and enjoying your surroundings.

When it's time to execute, do so with focus and conviction. You will play better; which obviously, in turn, helps you enjoy your round more. When you are out of your routine, enjoy your surroundings, that is after all, one of the main reasons you play the game; isn't it?

If, at the end of the round, you can truthfully say to yourself that you committed to and did the best you could on each and every shot; you have scored the best round you could possibly have scored on that given day. I guarantee, your scores will significantly improve without new clubs or a new swing the better you get at committing and focusing through a routine. It is no easy task to execute every shot throughout a round with full focus, commitment, and no distractions internally or externally, especially when you are first trying to implement a pre shot routine, but it will get easier, it will help, and you **will** get better.

Model Grip and Set UP Position

Now that you have a positive frame of mind and are ready to get on with the process of migrating and putting together your puzzle, we will start with the most influential part of any golf swing, good or bad; your' grip and set up positions. Your set up as a whole will determine what must be done throughout your swing to create a desired shot. Therefore, if there is a flaw in your setup there must be a, or series of, compensations at some point to correct that flaw and any other it may have created.

If you are physically capable of making a model swing, this will detract from the power, accuracy, and consistency of any golf swing to the degree of the flaw. In other words, it is extremely important to set up as soundly as possible.

The following model is the one I use to hit a straight golf shot with a normal trajectory. I will deviate from it only as is necessary considering a persons' physical limitations or if the student desires a particular shot shape that is not straight or of normal trajectory.

Grip is the first thing I look at in any swing. It is, after all, the only connection you have to the golf club, which is in turn the only connection you have to the ball. If you do not hold the club properly, your wrists will not work properly and you must make compensations with your body and arms to try and square the clubface and/or create power.

If there was only one thing I could change in your swing and your grip was flawed, your grip would be my adjustment. I would create a functioning grip and let your swing adapt to it. With a proper grip your golf swing must work at least somewhat properly to hit respectable shots. Assuming your proper grip is kept through good shots and bad shots alike, over time, your swing will improve as you intuitively try to hit controlled golf shots.

The same will happen when a grip is flawed. Intuitively, a person will subconsciously do what is necessary to try and get the golf ball to go in the direction desired. The problem here is that a flawed grip requires a flawed or compensated swing. The two negatives may occasionally hit shots that end up at the target desired {not likely}, but if so not with the same ease or power and typically not with the same consistency of a swing that is influenced by a good grip.

Over time, bad grips and the compensations they require will not only lead to less than your best in performance, but can also lead to injury. I have heard countless times that playing golf causes back problems. I could not disagree more; bad grips and set up positions that negatively influence swings are a great part of the injury problem. So, let's use a proper grip and set up in an effective way that will encourage your swing to be influenced positively rather than negatively.

Grip

Place the middle digit of your left hand forefinger on the underside of the grip. Now place the muscle pad just below your wrist and above your pinkie finger on top side of the grip {achieve this by "arching" your wrist up and not by rotating your hand {Fig. 5 – 1}. Place the left side of your left thumb in the center of the shaft and close your hand {Fig. 5 – 2}. From this position {without leaning} you should be able to see at least 2 but not more than 3 knuckles on your left hand. The "V" formed between your thumb and forefinger should point to your right shoulder. You should feel full and secure contact with the grip.

An easy way to achieve this position is to let your left hand comfortably hang by your left hip. Hold the grip of the club in your fingers and get a feel for it as described above {Fig. 5 – 3}. Try to do this without looking and trying to perfectly "place" your hand in the correct position, but close your eyes and feel the position described above. Make sure that the shaft of the club and the leading edge of the club face form a straight line {this is true when the club is in the position to your side, but not necessarily when in front of you addressing the ball depending on the ball position and club being used}. Spend some time doing this and soon it will become second nature and feel quite comfortable. When you get your left hand on the club properly, your right hand is fairly easy to fit.

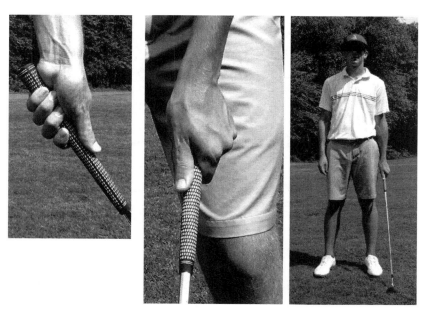

Fig. 5 – 1   Fig. 5 – 2   Fig. 5 - 3

Choose one of three basic ways to connect your hands:

- ■ - the interlocking grip – your right hand pinkie fits in between your forefinger and your middle finger of your left hand, interlocking {Fig. 5 – 4}

- ■ - the overlapping grip - your right hand pinkie simply lays on top of the groove made by your left forefinger and middle finger {Fig. 5 – 5}

- ■ - the ten finger grip - your right hand pinkie grips the grip side by side with your left hand forefinger. {Fig. 5 – 6}

Choose the one that feels most comfortable, powerful, and controllable to you. The way you choose to connect your hands is a preference. The relationship they have to the club face is what matters.

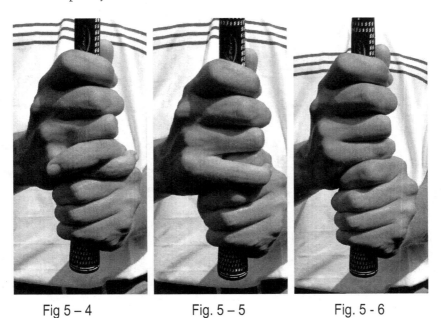

Fig 5 – 4   Fig. 5 – 5   Fig. 5 - 6

Now place your right hand on the grip so that the middle digit of your right forefinger is on the underside of the grip and the lifeline of your right hand fits onto your left thumb. If there were an eye in the palm of your right hand, it would be looking parallel left of the target line. The right side of your right thumb should now rest on the center of the grip and the "V" now formed by your right hand thumb and forefinger is also pointing to your right shoulder. Once again, it does not matter if you overlap, interlock, or ten finger grip the club, the relationship is the same and is what really matters. {Fig. 5 – 7 and 7a}

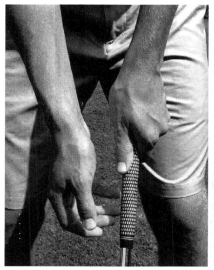

Fig. 5 – 7   Fig. 5 – 7a

I am going to measure the amount of grip pressure on a scale from 1 to 10, 10 being as hard as you can grip the club. I like to see the pressure in your hands range from 4 to 6. Too light in the 0 to 3 range and you will have less control of the club and tend to tighten and change pressure during the swing. Too tight in the 7 to 10 range and you will create too much tension, making a rhythmical swing and releasing the club very difficult. The 4 to 6 range will allow you to control the club and release it as well. It is important to me that the pressure in your hands is equal for your left hand and right. They should play equal roles, neither one dominating. More than people realize, your grip actually influences the way you set up the rest of your body. If you have followed the guidelines above, you are already positively affecting the rest of your set up and believe it or not, even your swing. Let's look at some other parts of your set up that play a very influential role in your golf swing.

Feet Position (angle relative to target line & width)

The angle at which you place your feet is extremely important and is often times overlooked. Assuming your weight remains balanced in your feet (not rolling to the outside or inside of your foot) your foot position

influences how much your hips can turn which influences how much your shoulders can turn, relative to your flexibility. If your trailing foot (right foot for a right handed player) is turned out too far, you will tend to over turn in your backswing and restrict your forward swing. If your forward foot is turned out too much to the target, your backswing will be restricted and you will tend to "spin out" {This means you may clear or turn your hips just fine, but out of sequence, before you get your weight into your forward foot} or "slide" in your forward swing {this means laterally moving past the ball without rotation}. It is simply more difficult to hit into a firm left side when your left foot is turned out too far. So, my ideal position is setting up feet that are "square" or in other words "perpendicular to the target line" {Fig. 5 – 8)

Fig. 5 – 8

I think the trailing foot and right knee are the "cornerstones" of the entire golf swing. They are what control the coiling of the backswing and should be pointing fairly, if not exactly, straight forward {perpendicular to the target line}. At the top of your backswing, if your weight has remained balanced throughout your right foot and your knee has maintained its' flex and points in front of your toes, your hips will have turned the proper amount (approximately half or slightly less than half as much as your shoulders) relative to your flexibility. For your forward swing you will now have a solid platform, away from which you can drive through the ball, to the target and to a balanced finish.

The physical limitations one has will determine how much is acceptable for each foot to be turned. Again, I like feet to be as square as possible, but will adjust as the students body type, flexibility, or other physical limitations dictate. That being said, I prefer to see a swing that is shorter with good foot and leg position than one that is longer but loses its' coil, posts, and soundness because of flared feet.

The width you place your feet is also very important, too close together and you risk losing your balance; too far apart and you make pivoting require too much lateral movement. I like to see feet placed in the range from hip width to shoulder width {Fig. 5 – 8}. An easy way to guide yourself is to dangle a club from your right shoulder and then from your left to see the positioning of your feet relative to your shoulders and hips {Fig. 5 – 9}.

Fig. 5 - 9

Weight distribution in feet

Weight distribution should be even throughout your feet. The balance of your body should be in an athletic and ready position. If your weight gets to the outside, to the heels, or to the toes of your feet; balance, consistency, and power will be very difficult to achieve as you will be seeking balance throughout your swing. This makes creating the most powerful and properly sequenced swing to your highest potential almost, if not impossible.

As for percentage of weight back foot to front foot, on a straight forward golf shot on a fairly level lie, I like to see your weight fifty percent right and fifty percent left.

Alignment

Always aim the club face first and then aim yourself to the clubface. This will greatly increase your ability to line up properly consistently. The chapter on pre shot routine goes over how to do this more in depth.

A line across your feet, hips, shoulders, arms, and eyes should all be parallel left of the target line (the line across your feet should actually be visualized from your heels, but if your feet are straight forward your toe line is fine). You can use the old image of a railroad track; the ball sits on the rail furthest from you and a line across your feet, hips, shoulders, eyes, and arms are parallel to the one you are standing on {Fig. 5 – 10}.

Fig. 5 – 10

A great way to practice alignment is on a wooden deck with the parallel boards. You can get fantastic feedback from all of the parallel lines. Pick a target, aim the clubface, and then set up with your body lines perpendicular to the clubface and parallel to the lines in the deck {Fig 5 – 11}. To help with your shoulders or hips, just put the club in your hands across either and adjust until it is parallel to the boards {Fig. 5 – 12}. Do this over and over to help you visually get a sense for being properly aligned. You can do this anywhere there are parallel lines even on the kitchen floor please don't swing in the kitchen if you have a wife or mother in the house.

| Fig. 5 – 11 | Fig. 5 - 12 |

Ball Position

Ball position is often over looked, but is crucial to solid ball striking and starting the ball on line.

There are two main ways to determine ball position. One way is a constant ball position off the forward heel with varying foot widths. The shorter and more lofted the club, the narrower the stance. The longer and less lofted the club, the wider the stance up to shoulder width.

The way I choose, moves the ball position and maintains a fairly constant foot width. Your wedges {the most lofted clubs} will be played at and slightly left of the center of your heels. The longer and less lofted your club becomes, the more forward to the instep of your forward foot your ball position will move. The following are in order left to right, a wedge, a six iron, and a 1 wood/metal {Fig. 5 – 13, 14, and 15}.

Fig. 5 – 13   Fig. 5 – 14   Fig. 5 – 15

There are times when you may need to play the ball slightly outside of these parameters, but not when playing a normal straight forward shot on a flat lie. Ball position will move around a bit when the lie is not flat {depending on the severity of the slope, more forward going uphill and more back going downhill or if the lie is down in deeper grass, ball position may move a little back}.

How far your hands are away from your body (how far away from the ball you stand) will be greatly influenced by your posture. Once you have proper posture your arms should comfortably hang under your shoulders and approximately one spread hands width away from your belt line {Fig. 5 – 16}. Another easy way to check this is to get into your set up position and then take your right hand off of the grip and let your arm hang. If your hand does not move out or in, you are a good distance from the ball {Fig. 5 – 17}. If it moves out toward the ball, you are too close and if it moves in toward you, you are too far away.

Fig. 5 - 16   Fig. 5 - 17

Posture

Most people tend to droop or squat in posture because of comfort, fatigue, lack of strength, or lack of knowledge about how to stand. Try and get as close to this model as your body will allow, as posture influences a golf swing much more than people give it credit.

Once you have your foot position, stand straight up at attention with the club in front of you {Fig. 5 – 18}. Then, from your hips {not your shoulders}, bend forward with your back straight until your arms and hands hang approximately one spread hands width away from your belt line and comfortably under your shoulders. Your chest will face slightly above the ball. The middle of your hips should still be over your ankles {Fig. 5 – 19}. Now, slightly flex your knees making sure to keep your weight in the middle of your feet and the middle of your hips over your ankles {Fig. 5 – 20}. You should feel athletic and balanced. Make sure your head is up {does not mean arched back}; this will help straighten your spine and help maximize your ability to turn and coil without lifting.

| Fig. 5 – 18 | Fig. 5 – 19 | Fig. 5 – 20 |

In simple terms...rear up, chest over, and let your arms hang, slightly flex your knees. Your weight is in the middle of your feet.

An easy way to check your posture is to get into your set up position {Fig. 5 – 21}, lift up your body maintaining its' relationship on the balls of your feet {Fig. 5 – 22}, then lower back down {Fig. 5 – 23}. When your heels hit the ground, you are in position.

Fig. 5 - 21   Fig. 5 – 22   Fig. 5 – 23

Hand Position

As was mentioned in the posture section your hands should hang comfortably under your shoulders. If you have the proper grip, posture, and distance from the ball they will be at the correct height; but where should they be in relation to the ball, in front of, even with, or behind the ball?

I think the easiest answer to this question is to form a straight line from your leading shoulder to the ball with your arm and shaft of your club

{Fig. 5 – 24}. If you were to error I would like to see hands **slightly** behind what would be a straight line {Fig. 5 – 25}. This encourages the golf club to stay more in front of you and swing away in harmony with your hands, arms, and shoulders.

Fig. 5 – 24   Fig. 5 - 25

Head Position

Another overlooked position of the setup and swing is your head position. The angle in which you hold your head from start to finish will heavily influence how far back you can turn and your ability to maintain a simple "1" back "2" through swing.

If your head tilts toward your target you will overturn, lose coil, and lift. This will make you force the club back to the ball with your shoulders or stress your back to very unhealthy limits, neither of which is desirable in my mind.

Keep a line across your eyes perpendicular to your spine or your nose in line with your spine. You grip with your right hand lower than your left so there is a slight tilt of your spine to the right, which means your head will also "slightly" tilt {relative to vertical} to maintain a normal relationship as well. Use a mirror to see the relationship your head has with your spine. You can see the correct relationship in any of the face on pictures in this chapter {Fig. 5 – 24 and 25}.

It is ok if your head "slightly" swivels around your spine, just no tilting back to the target {Fig. 6 – 11}.

Summary

Your set up influences your swing more than you may think, so take the time to check it on a regular basis. It will only take a few minutes every week to reinforce what a proper set up looks like from your perspective. Once you have a solid setup, bad set up positions do not just appear overnight. They creep in and over time appear to be normal because of their subtle migration.

Always, make sure to "SET YOURSELF UP" for success.

The Full Swing

This is a tricky one. Teaching effective golf swings through text or even through video is, at the very least, EXTREMELY difficult. The person writing or talking cannot see your set up positions, swing motions and tendencies, or your attitude. He cannot see or hear from you what your physical limitations and capabilities are or if you have pain. He does not know your desire to improve or your level of commitment. There are many factors that need to be considered and prioritized that the writer or speaker does not have access to, so there is NOTHING like good ole fashioned hands on (hand for me :) instruction by a qualified Teaching Professional. That being said….get as close as you can to the set up described in the Set Up Chapter and follow the three things I stress in this chapter, letting your body tell you how long your swing should be, and you will have a great chance of hitting solid on line golf shots with power consistently.

Golf swings are extremely complicated yet deceptively simple motions and can be made as complicated as one likes or as simple. I think they are sadly over complicated on a regular basis. At the time of this writing, I have been playing golf for 37 + years, a professional for 24 +, and a Master Professional for 10 +. In that time I have learned that I see more, faster and clearer, and say less, slower and more repetitive. In other words…. I have simplified my method to a few key concepts and thoughts that I prioritize, once you are set up properly as described in the Set Up Chapter. To me, it all boils down to a simple load, push, and release; a turn of your shoulders, a push of your right hip and knee to the target, and timing the rotation of the clubface.

My swing model is, in my mind; the easiest, most efficient, powerful, and consistent way to move a golf ball straight or with a controlled bend in either direction. This does not mean that I reinvented the wheel and it is "mine", but it is what I personally have concluded and chosen to prioritize through my experiences over 37 + years of playing, practicing and teaching. I have been influenced by many teachers, but most of all, by the results my students have gotten and experiences with 'trial and error" in my own swing. It is simply what works; not only for me but everyone I have ever worked with that did it. No one is ever perfect every time, but the more you understand and the closer to the model you migrate, the better the results.

I can only wish that I had the understanding of what I should have been doing when I was 20 that I do now. I try to get my students as close to the model in my mind as their physical ability will allow. If there are physical limitations, of course adjustments must be made, but only if absolutely necessary. I prefer to make modifications to my model rather than compensations and prefer those modifications to be only in range of motion. A shorter efficient swing is better to me any day than a longer one with compensations.

It is simple geometry and that cannot be argued. How to make that geometry take place on a consistent basis is an argument/discussion that has been had and probably always will be had by many teachers that have different models, motions, and positions that they choose to prioritize. Hopefully, we all continue to grow and simplify our views, through education both learned and experienced and better communication, so that golf is at some point not considered to be the hardest and most frustrating sport to play, but the most enjoyable and easier to learn than in times gone by.

To me, the ideal swing has a path that touches the target line but does not cross it and a timing of face rotation that is square to that path. Depending on the club, it will have a bottom of swing/arc that is at and after the ball for the most lofted clubs, at the ball for middle lofted clubs and just before and at the ball for the least lofted clubs. Ball position will take care of that. Achieving this ideal path, face rotation, and bottom of swing is what my model produces and what I strive for, but in the end it is simply about matching path and release {see the Reading Ball Flight Chapter}.

Great golf has been played with MANY different combinations of path and release that matched to produce a consistent shot pattern. However, I am of the opinion that "that" golf could have been even greater if those players had a path and release that would allow them to hit a ball straight, which allows for more ease and consistency bending the ball in both directions. When you have that kind of control, no architect, greens keeper, or committee can hide a pin from you or intimidate you from the teeing area. The model I use allows that.

Fig. 6 - 1

So....here we go with the three key points of that model, after a solid set up position is established, for a right handed player {just flip the words right and left if you are left handed}.

As you may have read in this book.... :) our set up is the beginning to being consistent, efficient, and powerful. It is also the first piece of The PuzzleDuck and heavily influences what must be done in your swing to produce an effective golf shot. So, our first priority is a proper set up to encourage consistent, efficient, and powerful motions. Once in a solid set up position and a complete balanced swing can be made with a finish position in balance {Fig. 6 – 1} {this in its' own right corrects many flaws}, I choose to correct the path of the swing first and the release of the clubface second. When the club is swung on the correct path, the proper release of the clubface is encouraged and is much easier to achieve and time.

The following swing sequence is the base model that I use for every golf shot and club. {Fig. 6 – 2a, 3a, 4a, 5a, 6a, 7a, 8a, 9a} and {Fig. 2b, 3b, 4b, 5b, 6b, 7b, 8b, 9b}

Fig. 6 – 2a   Fig. 6 – 3a   Fig. 6 – 4a

Fig. 6 – 5a   Fig. 6 – 6a   Fig. 6 – 7a

Fig. 6 – 8a   Fig. 6 – 9a

Fig. 6 – 2b

Fig. 6 – 3b

Fig. 6 – 4b

Fig. 6 – 5b

Fig. 6 – 6b

Fig. 6 – 7b

Fig. 6 – 8b   Fig. 6 – 9b

Again…assuming a solid set up is achieved and a full and balanced swing can be made, I have stream lined my thinking to three basic parts of a swing {the remaining three pieces of The PuzzleDuck}. There are many little things that I look for and notice that affect and influence a swing, but it is simply not possible to cover them all without confusing us both. A few are listed at the end of this chapter. The, three main focuses of mine are what follow. Get better with each concept in order. Your setup influences them all, the first influences the second and the second the third. I have noticed that I repeat the same statements over and over both in writing and teaching. The older I get the tighter and cleaner my message, but like a broken record over and over. Keep it simple, set up properly, load, push, and release.

First - Load – This means to load your back leg. To coil against a braced back leg

- How to do it – Turn your shoulders "level" away from your target against a **braced** right leg until your body says "you cannot go anymore" {Fig. 6 – 2a/b, 3a/b, 4a/b, and 5a/b}. Focus on your left shoulder and turn only as far your flexibility will allow without something "breaking" down. Think to turn your left shoulder to your right foot or behind the ball and feel a coil into your right leg. Your shoulders should actually turn perpendicular to your spine, but feel level {Fig. 6 – 3b, 4b, and 5b}.

- "Breaking down" could be your right leg straightening, your weight moving to the outside edges of your foot, your head tilting to the target or rotating too far, lifting or tilting back to the target, your left arm bending too much, your left wrist cupping, or your hands letting go of the grip and opening. **Your body's range of motion and flexibility dictates how long your golf swing is**. Length of swing is over rated. This shorter swing {Fig. 6 – 10} is better than this longer, but broken down swing {Fig. 6 - 11} ......all day every day.

Fig. 6 – 10   Fig. 6 – 11

- Your shoulders turn the club away and your lower body reacts. Thinking of your left shoulder may help you. There is no pulling, rolling of your forearms, or lifting of the club away, simply turn your shoulders and let your wrists set the club. Your left wrist should cock up **flat** {Fig. 6 – 4a/b and 5a/b}. This will put the shaft on "about" a 45 degree angle from the ground just over halfway back, assuming you have the grip we described in the Set Up Chapter. A compact efficient coil is what I like to see {Fig. 6 – 5a and b}

- Do not worry about your arms......if you cock your wrists with your left one flat they will be just fine. Your hands and club will be "deep" as your left arm lines up with your shoulders {Fig. 6 – 5b}. Again, no pulling, rolling of your forearms, or lifting the club away from the ball, simply turn your left shoulder to your right foot against a **braced** right leg and set/cock your wrists.

Things to look for and feel –

- $The **"corner stone"** of the entire swing is, in my opinion, your back foot, knee, and hip. This part of your body does NOT move in your backswing, **it braces.** Your knee and foot should not move at all and your hip only reacts to the turn of your shoulders. This part of your body does not "float" out, nor straighten, nor flex more, but **braces.** Your weight should stay evenly distributed throughout your foot, if not slightly to the inside {Fig. 6 – 5a/b}.$

- Let your head move a little to the right, it's **OK.** Be athletic. This does not mean

- 6 inches, but an inch or two is fine as you turn against your braced leg. Up, down, backwards or forwards is not so good, but a little right and left is fine by me.

- Again, your shoulders actually turn perpendicular to your spine angle, but **feel** level {Fig. 6 – 3b, 4b, and 5b}. We DO NOT wish to see your shoulders turning "down".

- Turn **only** as far as your flexibility will allow. This is until something has to "break down" to go any further. In my book, a shorter compact swing {Fig. 6 – 10} is without question better than one too long and "breaking down" {Fig. 6 – 11}.

Drills that will help –

- Arms across your chest drill
- Making swings with only your arms
- The Grip Down Drill – part 1
- Push a 2 by 4 away from ball in backswing

- 1 – 2 Static Drill – part 1
- Pre set wrist and swing drill
- Slow motion swings
- Super slow motion swings

Second – Push –This means to start/sequence your forward swing with a "push" to the target, from your braced and coiled against right hip, knee, and foot. Again, to the target, not out in the direction of the ball. Move the club forward with your right hip, knee, and foot; not your shoulders and/or arms.

How to do it – Push your weight into and around a planted left foot and braced left leg {Fig. 6 – 6a/b and 7 – 7a/b}. This is done with your right hip, knee, and foot; keeping your right knee flexed. Push your right hip and knee to the target keeping your right knee flexed. Push your right hip {pant pocket} past where the ball is, keeping your right knee flexed. Did I just repeat myself three times? :) Getting your right hip past where the ball is at impact is not going to happen if your left leg is firm and your weight is balanced in your left leg and foot….but a thought/feeling.

It is a sequenced and blended motion toward the target that starts from your right hip, knee, and foot. Your shoulders and arms will react and "fall/follow" into place so that they can contribute through impact and thru to your finish. The relationship between the shaft, your arms, and shoulders will not change {Fig 6 – 5a/b and 6a/b} until the weight of the club head and your right side release through impact.

Use your right side. As a right handed player, it is your' most coordinated, most powerful, and the side with the most feel. So, use it. Hit with it in the correct sequence. Move the club forward with your right foot, knee, and hip; and hit/drive through with your whole right side to a complete and balanced finish position.

Things to look for and feel –

- Your shoulders and arms WILL react and follow properly if they do nothing and follow until they release through impact {Fig. 6 – 6a/b}. They DO NOT lead. They will ONLY "hang" behind if your weight "hangs" behind. There is no "pulling down". Let your upper body react to the forward push of your right hip, knee, and foot and hit through impact….Do less….get more.

- Starting with your right foot, knee, and hip….get your weight left and your right side thru the ball to a balanced finish position! The only way to get through the ball in the proper sequence is to first load your back leg and then to "push" off of that loaded back leg to the target. If you wish to feel the proper sequence….. simply through a rock.

- There should be very little {if any} pressure in your back foot at impact {Fig. 6 -7a/b}

- Keep moving your right side through impact into and around your braced forward foot and leg to a full balanced finish position {Fig. 6 – 9a/b}.

- Keep your head up and get your right side through the ball in the proper sequence.

Drills that will help –

- Arms across your chest drill

- The Grip Down Drill – part 3

- Forward hand on top of a club and trailing hand swinging under

- 1 – 2 Static Drill

- The Belt Loop Drill

- The Step Drill

- The Club Throwing Drill

- One Arm Right Arm Drill

- Step Through Drill

- Knock Down Shots

- Impact Position Drill

- Weed Whackin Drill

- Making A Station Drill

- Slow Motion Swings

- Super Slow Motion Swings

Third – Release – This means to "rotate" the club. A golf club is designed to rotate and has "released" when its' toe passes its' heel relative to the path it is swung on {Fig. 6 – 12, 13, and 14}.

Fig. 6 – 12   Fig. 6 – 13   Fig. 6 - 14

How to do it – Rotate the club through the impact area with your forearms. This does NOT mean trying to square the clubface with your shoulders. Your forearms are the most simple to think of because they can only move in two directions, right and left, and they are actually the part of you that does the rotating. Believe me, this I know. :)
{Fig. 6 – 15, 16, and17}.

71

| Fig. 6 – 15 | Fig. 6 – 16 | Fig. 6 - 17 |

If thinking of your hands is easier for you, so be it. Just be careful to keep your wrists out of the motion. They can move in many undesirable directions. Your hands only hold the club and feel, but if thinking of them makes releasing the club properly, easier for you, then think of them, making sure your left wrist stays flat. That being said…..focus on your forearms. :)

Things to look for and feel –

- When your sequence forward is started from your right foot, knee, and hip pushing your weight into and around a solid left foot and leg {not your shoulders or arms} your arms will be pulled into the correct path {Fig. 6 – 6b} and make your arms and club release more naturally with less effort and easier to time.

- Your left elbow should point behind you through impact {Fig. 6 – 18} and down as your arms rotate and release {Fig. 6 - 19}.

Fig. 6 - 18   Fig. 6 – 19

- Assuming the previous two thoughts {load and push} are being done correctly, the path of your swing will be touching your target line, but not crossing it, which gives your ball a very good chance of starting on line. It is now simply a matter of timing the rotation of the club face. If your balls are going to the left.......you are rotating the club too soon.....if they are going to the right.......you are rotating too late........if they are going straight.............that's a good thing. Refer to the Reading Ball Flight Chapter.

Drills that will help –

- Making swings with only your arms
- The Grip Down Drill – parts 2, 3, and 4
- Swinging up high and swinging from your knees
- Split Grip Drill
- One Arm Left Arm Drill
- Set, Rotate, and Swing
- Slow Motion Swings
- Super Slow Motion Swings

Summary

Set up properly, turn your shoulders level to the right against a braced right leg letting your left wrist cock up flat, push your weight and right hip through "to the target", and time the release/rotation of the club. It really can be that simple........Turn level to the right against a braced right leg, move the club through with your right hip, knee, and foot, and time the rotation of the clubface. Load, push, and release. Your flexibility will determine your length of swing.

A few things to be aware of and keep in mind:

- Set up properly. Get on the back side of the golf club and ball....The correct grip is best, but grip too far in your fingers and to the right before too much in your palms and to the left.

- Balance – being able to swing in balance and holding your finish position will tell you a lot about the efficiency of your swing, your effort level, and give you your best chance to be consistent. A balanced finish position consists of your right foot vertical with its' shoelaces facing your target as well as your hips and shoulders. Your body should be vertical and in balance over your left leg with the club balanced in your hands over your left shoulder {Fig. 6 – 9a/b}. In reality, your laces and body are facing parallel left, but to keep it is simple...think, to the target.

- Use the ground. Feel the pressure of your body in your right leg in your backswing and your left in your through swing. That's why we have spikes....grip the ground...use it to push to the target. This does not mean "thrust out".....but driving your right hip and knee to the target.

- When struggling......Check your set up and **SLOW** down. Be aware of your breathing. Breathing properly will help you get control of your rhythm and the harmony of your swing. If you are breathing shorter and faster than normal.....consciously take **deeper** and **slower** breaths to slow your body down as well as your thinking. By deep, I mean to the bottom of your lungs. In through your nose and out through your mouth.

- Rhythm – this is swinging with all of "you" moving in harmony. There is no one part "outrunning" another. Your whole swinging motion is blending together and flowing at a consistent and smooth pace. Some swings are faster than others, but all efficient swings are in harmony and have rhythm.

- Maintain constant contact with your grip. No gaps. This does not mean to squeeze harder, but to maintain constant connection throughout your swing until the very end. This is a big deal. :)

- A short swing with technique is better than a long swing that breaks down. Let your flexibility determine the length.

- **Brace that right leg!**

- Your right leg never straightens in a golf swing.

- Get left! Get through! Always think "**through**" the ball and not "down" or "at" the ball.

- Keep your nose in line with your spine, both in backswing and through swing. Your spine tilts slightly to the right, because your right hand is lower than your left in your grip and your ball position, so your head should also tilt the same amount {Fig. 6 – 2a, 3a, 4a, 5a, 6a, 7a, 8a}. Your head position relative to your spine is a significant influence to many aspects of your swing.

- Firm grip, soft arms. This means a grip pressure that is about a 5 on a 10 scale for control and that your arms are soft but, ready and reactive.

- Your right elbow points to the ground in your backswing {Fig. 6 – 4b and 5b}, and your left elbow down in your through swing {Fig. 6 – 19 and 1}. This does not mean to tuck them, but to support with them, which encourages your forearms to work properly.

- Don't be scared to let your head move a little right and left; not up, down, backwards, or forwards, but slightly right going back and slightly left going through is a good thing in my eyes. Be athletic.

- Be aware of your effort level. You would ideally like to play in the 75 to 85% range. Do the Effort Level Awareness Drill to understand and be aware of your effort levels at all times. Breathe.

- A golf swing is a blended motion that moves in harmony back and through.....1 back {Fig. 6 – 5a}......2 through {Fig. 6 – 9a}. When the club goes to the right....your weight goes to the right.....when your weight goes left....your club goes left. You should be able to turn to the right, stop at the top of your backswing and hold that position in balance with no trouble. Then push through to a complete balanced finish position and be able to hold that position in balance with no trouble as well. 1 back.......2 through.

- Think "THROUGH" the ball, not "DOWN" or "AT" the ball. Didn't I already say that? :)

- Keep your head up and follow the ball with your eyes. Do **not** keep your head down!

- If you are hitting behind the ball or hitting thin shots....make sure your set up is correct, your back leg is braced, that you are not over turning in your backswing, and that you are getting to your forward leg soon enough.

- No one ever has or ever will strike every shot perfect. The object is to understand why the ball goes where it goes and tighten up the misses so they are manageable. Accept the FACT that you are going to strike many more imperfect shots than perfect shots and have some fun......delete the bad ones and file the good ones forever.

- **SMILE! LIGHTEN UP! Hit it, chase it, hit again....til it's in the hole....enjoy the JOURNEY!**

Reading Ball Flight & Matching the Clubface To Your Swing Path

This chapter is not meant to change your swing. It is only to help you understand what will make your swing as is produce a ball flight that is more under control. That does not mean I do not think you should try to improve your swing, only that no matter what your swing looks like you need to understand the two things that tell the ball where to go, path and release. Path is the direction in which the club is swung and release is when the clubface rotates through a square to the path position.

One of the biggest breakthroughs for me, regarding control of my ball flight, was understanding path of swing and the release or rotation of the clubface. There are many things that influence path and release, but just understanding the following basic information was a great help.

There are many combinations between the path of the club and the angle of the clubface at impact. For me, the ideal combination is a club that is swung and touches, but does not cross the target line {down the line} with a clubface that is released squarely at impact to produce a straight shot {Fig. 7 – 7, 8, and 9}. However, many combinations will work. Understanding this relationship between path and release of the clubface allows one to begin to control his ball.

Most people swing out to in {Fig. 7 – 1, 2, and 3},

| Fig. 7 – 1 | Fig. 7 – 2 | Fig. 7 - 3 |

Some people swing in to out {Fig. 7 – 4, 5, and 6},

| Fig. 7 – 4 | Fig. 7 – 5 | Fig. 7 - 6 |

Even fewer people swing down the line and touch but don't cross the target line
{Fig. 7 – 7, 8, and 9}.

Fig. 7 – 7   Fig. 7 – 8   Fig. 7 - 9

The amount the club is swung from out to in or in to out must be offset by a clubface angle that will cause the ball to curve back to the target the correct amount. If the angle of the clubface does not match the path, the ball will not curve enough or will curve too far. This can get somewhat confusing, so I am going to explain it the way I see it and teach it. It is quite simple if you let it be so. The path of your swing tells the ball the direction in which to start and the club face tells the ball where to end up. There can, of course, be exceptions as in anything else, but in my experience those exceptions would have to be extreme, especially if you have a respectable grip.

Simply put, with a good grip, when you swing to the right of your target {Fig. 7 – 4, 5, and 6}, the ball will start to the right of your target; when you swing to the left of your target {Fig. 7 – 1, 2, and 3}, the ball will start to the left of your target; and when you swing to your target {Fig. 7 – 7, 8, and 9}, the ball has a chance of starting at and going straight to your target. The ball will go straight to your target only if you swing down the target line {the club touches, but does not cross the target line} and the clubface is square to that path.

The timing of the release of the clubface will tell the ball where to end up. Golf clubs are designed to rotate or "release", not move in straight lines. The clubface has released when the toe of the club passes by the heel of the club relative to the path it is swung on {Fig. 7 – 10, 11, and 12}.

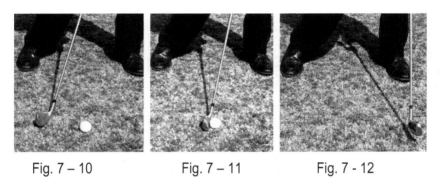

Fig. 7 – 10   Fig. 7 – 11   Fig. 7 - 12

If the clubface is released before impact it will be closed at impact {Fig. 7 – 13} and the ball will start close to the path of the swing and then curve to the left the amount it is closed. If it is released at impact {Fig. 7 – 14} the ball will go straight on that path. If it is released after impact it will be open at impact {Fig. 7 – 15} and the ball will start close to the path of the swing and then curve to the right the amount it is open.

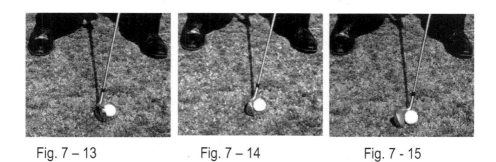

| Fig. 7 – 13 | Fig. 7 – 14 | Fig. 7 - 15 |

When I teach, once I have created a sound set up and grip in a student, I tend to improve the path of a swing first and then the clubface. It has been my experience that a club swung on the correct path encourages the club to release more naturally, which makes timing the release much easier to learn and do.

In order to time your release properly, you must first know where you tend to swing relative to your target, so let's go over a few simple ways to find out.

Reading the flight of your ball will tell you in which direction you are swinging and your timing of the release of the clubface. Always identify a specific target. As stated above, if the ball starts to the right of your target {Fig. 7 – 16}, you are swinging to the right. If it starts at your target {Fig. 7 – 17}, you are swinging to your target and if it starts to the left of your target {Fig. 7 – 18}, you are swinging left.

Fig. 7 – 16   Fig. 7 - 17   Fig. 7 - 18

You can also tell the path you tend to swing on by looking at your divots. Hit a few shots with a 7 iron and if you take divots, observe the direction in which your divots tend to go relative to your target line {Fig. 7 – 19}. Divots can sometimes be difficult to read, and if they are, lay the shaft of your club along the divot and you can see where you are swinging relative to your target.

Fig. 7 – 19

If you do not take divots or are having trouble reading them, another good way to learn the path of your swing is to simply make some swings standing on a wooden deck. Aim along the lines of the boards and make some swings (just above the boards, of course :). Be sure to swing the way that is comfortable and how you normally do. Don't let the lines of the boards influence you. Watch the blur your club head makes. You should easily be able to see the path your club takes relative to the lines of the boards. {Fig. 7 – 20, 21, and 22}. This swing is "in to out" or to the right of the target line.

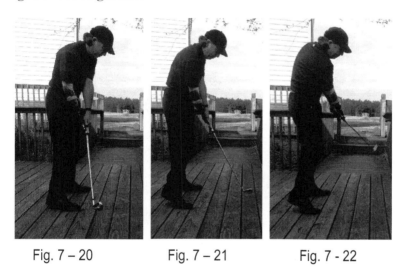

| Fig. 7 – 20 | Fig. 7 – 21 | Fig. 7 - 22 |

Once you know the path of your swing, the next question is, does your clubface release at the proper time for that path? If you have a sound grip and your ball tends to slice {curve to the right for a right handed player} too far, you need to release/rotate the clubface a little sooner. If it tends to hook {curve to the left for a right handed player} too far, you need to release/rotate the club face a little later. Just how much sooner or later is a matter of you fine tuning your timing of release relative to your path of swing.

To get your ball to find the target, the bottom line is; if you are swinging to the left of your target, at impact the club face must be open relative to the amount left you are swinging. If you are swinging to the right of your target, at impact the club face must be closed relative to the amount right you are swinging.

A great way to learn path and release is to try controlling the flight of your ball. Aim and swing to the left of a target; hold the face open the correct amount to make the ball curve back to the target. Firm up your grip just a little to help you. Many people will be able to do this relatively easily, because they already curve the ball this way. Then, aim and swing to the right of a target and release the face early enough to make the ball hook back to the target. Make sure your arms are soft enough to freely release/rotate the club. This will be more challenging for most, because releasing the clubface is not something many people do. You can feel this motion by doing "The Grip Down Drill" or "The Split Grip Drill" in the Drill Chapter.

Put a shaft or stick in the ground about ten paces out and in line with your target to help you visually see starting the ball left of your target and right of your target. Few people will be able to do this straight from the start, but as you practice, in time you will become more path and face aware. Do so with slow little swings from shoulder to shoulder to get a feel and build up the length and speed to normal over time.

When you can start your ball left of your target and curve it back and right of your target and curve it back, try to swing down the target line and hit some straight shots. You may be surprised at the control you have.

Again, there are many things that influence ones ability to swing in a given direction and release the club at the correct time, but if you understand the release of the clubface relative to your swing path you can control how much your ball curves. Even if your swing is not of tour quality, you can control the flight of your ball to a manageable degree.

Becoming path and face aware is extremely valuable to controlling your golf ball. Whether you play a left to right curve, right to left curve, or a straight shot, you must be able to match up the release to the path. No one will ever be able to match the path and face perfectly every time; we are human beings, not machines, and there are too many variables from wind to nerves that affect both. The best we can do is to minimize the margin of error through technique and timing. Just remember that, within reason, the path tells the ball where to start and the face tells it where to end up.

Putting; the Great Equalizer

In putting you can be as good as the best players in the world; if, you have a simple and sound technique, are willing to put in the time and effort to hone your skills, practice reading greens, and mentally believe in your ability. Putting is the simplest shot in golf. It has the fewest moving parts, the shortest motion, and uses the easiest club in the bag to hit solid; the putter. So, why is it so hard? Why do we make it so hard? Some of the most powerful people in the world get nervous under the pressure of making a simple three foot putt, yet can run a country, negotiate multi-million dollar deals, fly a jet plane, or complete a game winning pass on demand. Why is it so hard to get that little ball into that little hole?

The closer you get to the hole, the less room for error you have. You can be off line and distance with quite a buffer from the centerline of a fairway and even approaching a green, but at the cup the margin of error can be less than an inch. Putting is easy to do yet more difficult to master. There is very little wiggle room with speed or line if the ball is to go in. No one makes every putt, and with every missed makeable putt doubt entrenches itself in the normal person which in turn plays havoc with confidence, which plays havoc with nerves, which plays havoc with technique, which plays havoc with results. It is a vicious cycle.

I think people in general tend to put too much pressure on themselves to make putts. Simply trying too hard and putting too much value on a make or a miss. Not that you shouldn't expect to make every putt or are not trying to make every putt, but most people have unrealistic expectations. No one makes every putt, not even the best players in the world that practice almost every day. You have only one chance to choose the correct line and apply the correct speed to any given putt during a round.

This is not something that can be done exactly every time, there are many factors that influence a putt from mental, to physical, to chance.

The mental can influence the physical when you are under pressure, whether from an external force or internal; muscles tighten and a fluid stroke is compromised; concentration becomes more difficult, distractions are amplified; and second guessing diminishes commitment. All of these factors and more make making a fluid committed stroke difficult.

Even if you choose the correct line, apply the correct speed, and are able to make a fluid committed stroke, you are still at the mercy of the green itself. The imperfections that may or may not be readily noticeable, influence the ball more than you might think, as do the varying speeds of greens from course to course, day to day, and even green to green on some courses.

There are only two things that matter in a putt; speed and direction. Many factors influence these two things; slope, grass height, grass type, grain, moisture, your aim, the mechanics of your stroke, your nerves, your thought process, your eyes and how you use them, etc. Through effective practice you will be able to process more and more of these factors quickly and efficiently, but never to an exact science. All you can do is commit to a line, aim the putter face, and roll the ball to the best of your ability along that line with the correct speed. Chance will take over from there. The more consistently you roll your ball on the correct line with the correct speed the more putts you will make, but you will never make them all. You can expect to make them all, but when one does not go in you must accept that fact and move on.

You can improve your putting right now, by simply thinking better. By thinking better I mean to let go of the result. This does not mean to be hap hazard or not care, but to take the pressure off. If it goes in, great; if not, then so be it. Let it go. All you can do is try your best and then be done with it. One great line that an older character at the course I grew up on named Tom "Tip Toe" Taylor used to say is, "it ain't nothin but a putt". And so it is, "nothing but a putt". Some will go in, some will not, and I guarantee you that if you take the pressure off and let go of your expectations {especially the short ones} you will make more putts.

Next, most people do not read putts well. Not because they cannot read them, but because they do not practice reading them. Most people practice putt by simply going from hole to hole on the practice green and rarely reading the putt. If they do read the putt, they only do so for the first one and not for the second or third. This is a loss of a valuable opportunity to learn. The second and third read is when you can learn from the previous putt and apply that information to the next putt. I think you should never hit a putt {unless it is less than two feet long and you know it is straight} without reading it. This includes every putt on the practice green. The more putts you read the better at reading them you will become as you apply the feedback you get from each putt.

The next problem I see is aim. Most people aim too directly to the hole on breaking putts, not only because of putt reading skills, but because they look too directly at the hole and approach breaking putts on an extended line from the hole through the ball instead of an extended line on the line in which the ball must start in order to play the correct amount of break. You will tend to aim and stroke where you look, so if you do not use your eyes properly or approach the ball on the correct line, chances are you will set up playing too little break and swing too directly to the hole.

It all starts with reading putts properly, but does not end there. If you read the putt properly, but do not use your eyes correctly or approach the ball on the correct line you will not start the ball on the correct line consistently and will tend to start the ball too directly at the hole. If you play too direct a line to the hole your intuition will tell you to hit the ball hard enough to hold that line which is typically going to be too hard and in its own way starts to interfere with your distance control.

Learn to use your eyes properly by looking along the line the ball must roll on as you aim and approach the ball on that line. Your aim will improve and so will your ability to start the ball on line. This will in turn help your speed by playing a softer line.

Here is a simple way to help you get your ball started on the correct line and let the ball fall to the hole with the correct speed. It takes a little practice and patience to do consistently, but it will help you start your ball on a better line, in turn helping you control your speed, which minimizes three putts and helps you make more. :)

1st - Read your putt and commit to the line you have chosen. While reading the putt, let your eyes trace a line along the break to the hole. Do not look directly at the hole, but burn a line in the ground along the break line with your eyes. Approach the ball on an extension of that line and only when you have 100% commitment to that line {Fig. 8 – 1}. Over read the line before you under read it {allow for too much break, before too little} on medium length to longer putts. Tend to play shorter putts {5 feet and in} a little firmer with a more direct line to take some of the break away and help you stroke through the ball confidently.

Fig. 8 – 1

Fig. 8 – 2

2nd – Always aim the club face first {Fig. 8 - 2}. Try to pick a starting line as close to the ball as possible. It is simply easier to line up to something closer than farther away. Then set yourself up to the putter face and line chosen, not to the hole {unless it is a dead straight putt}. A line across your eyes, shoulders and arms should be perpendicular to the putter face and parallel to the line of putt. I encourage a stance that is also parallel to the line, but your eyes, shoulders and arms are most important.

3rd – This part really takes discipline and is not easy to do initially, but well worth the effort to get comfortable with. Again, burn a line with your eyes to the hole along the path the ball must take with the proper speed. Once you get to the hole, re burn the line back to the ball. Starting at the hole, tracing back to the ball, and then back to the hole is also ok. You can use the image of a florescent line, a painted line, or anything else that may help you visualize the curve. I like to think of burning the curve in {Fig. 8 – 3}. The only time you should look straight to the hole is if you have a dead straight putt, and even then your eyes should trace a line on the ground.

Fig. 8 – 3

4th – To the best of your ability, roll the putt along the line you have traced. If it goes in; great! If not, so what! I guarantee you that your dog or cat {if you do not have a dog or cat} someone, will still love you, so let it go {Fig. 8 – 4}. It will feel good to just let it go. Take the pressure off.

Fig 8 – 4

If you follow this process your chances of success will greatly improve, even with your existing stroke, but what if you had a simple and repeating stroke to go along with this thought process? I think putting strokes are over analyzed and over complicated. There is just not that much going on. Try following these guidelines to help you make a simple efficient stroke and compliment your new thought process.

Setup

There are so many functioning grips that there is no "one-way". I do, however like to see the grip of the club run up the lifeline of your hands, the back of your lead hand and the palm of your trailing hand parallel with the putter face, and your thumbs straight down the top of the grip {Fig. 8 – 5, 5a, 5b, 9, and 10}. This makes the shaft of the club and your forearms form a straight line, decreasing room for error by minimizing club face rotation and arc of stroke. A conventional reverse overlap grip {your left index finger laps outside your right hand {Fig. 8 – 6 and 7} is used most, but I think you should at least "try" putting with your left hand below your right.

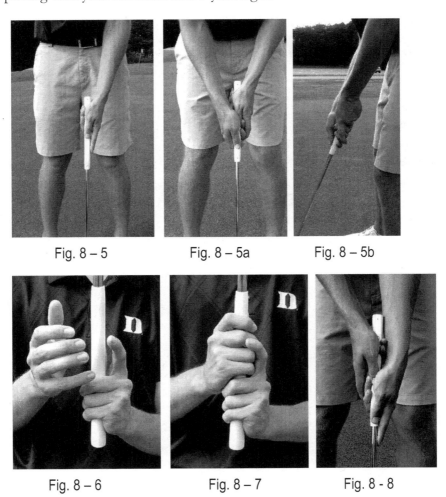

Fig. 8 – 5   Fig. 8 – 5a   Fig. 8 – 5b

Fig. 8 – 6   Fig. 8 – 7   Fig. 8 - 8

The grip I used most before I lost my hand is {Fig. 8 – 8}. I use basically the same grip now but just put the end of my right arm on the butt of the grip
{Fig. 8 – 3 and 12 thru 17}.

Grip pressure is important: too loose and you lose control of the club, too tight and you lose touch and feel. I tend to encourage a firm grip {on a scale from 1 to 10 – a 5 or 6}. Go with what gives you confidence, feels comfortable, and gets results, both in grip style and pressure.

Your eyes should be parallel to the target line, over the target line, and over the putter-head {Fig. 8 – 9 and 10}. Positioning your eyes parallel to and over the target line will help your shoulders line up parallel left of the target line. Your eyes over the putter head will put the deepest point of your swing just before the ball, allowing ball contact to be ever so slightly on your upswing {Fig. 8 – 10}. Contacting the ball as the club swings slightly upward will give the ball a truer roll, decreasing the chance for side spin and helping the ball stay on line, on the ground, giving it a purer roll.

Fig. 8 - 9   Fig. 8 - 10

- The length of putter you use or where you hold the putter should allow your arms to hang comfortably and freely under your shoulders. I do not like to see much bend in the elbows {Fig. 8 – 9 and 10}
- Your posture should be comfortable, but a straighter spine will encourage your back and shoulders to control the stroke more and your wrists less {Fig. 8 – 9}.
- The clubface should form right angles with the target line.
- A line across your eyes, shoulders, forearms, and feet should all be parallel to the target line. Ideally, your foot alignment will also be parallel, but it is less important than your arms, shoulders, and eyes; it is ok if you are more comfortable with them slightly open, closed, narrow or wide {Fig. 8 – 9 and 10}.
- Set up with the sole of the putter flat/flush with ground and ball in the center of the putter face {Fig. 8 – 11}.

It is optically easy to set up to the ball with it off center toward the toe. Off center strikes will rotate the clubface at impact and impart inconsistent energy to the ball influencing both distance and direction negatively.

Fig. 8 - 11

Stroke

Use your back and shoulders {not your arms and wrists}, turn the club approximately the same distance on both sides of the ball back and through. Slightly further in your forward stroke is good as you would like to have an accelerating stroke {Fig. 8 -12, 13, and 14}.

Fig. 8 – 12   Fig, 8 – 13   Fig. 8 - 14

Your stroke should resemble that of a pendulum on a slight arc. The club will work slightly inside the target line in your back stroke and again slightly inside the target line after impact. The club face should remain at right angles {square} to the natural arc of your stroke. The longer your stroke the more it will arc. Please, remember the arc is not manufactured but is minimal and a natural path produced by the angle created between the shaft and the club head
{Fig. 8 - 15, 16, and 17}.

| Fig. 8 – 15 | Fig. 8 – 16 | Fig. 8 - 17 |

There should be a rhythmic pace to your stroke. One that is not hurried or jerky {again, as a pendulum when it changes direction}. Make sure you swing the club far enough in your back swing that there I no need to rush your stroke forward, yet not too far that you feel the need to decelerate through impact.

Your wrists should be firm and have minimal movement. This does not mean tight and rigid, but firm enough to control the club and still have feel.

Make sure that the butt of the club and the head of the club always move proportionately in the same direction {Fig. 8 – 12, 13, and 14}.

One of the few "don'ts" in this book; but do not let the end of the grip move to the right as the head moves to the left {Fig. 8 – 18}. Move the head and the grip in the same direction so you stroke through the ball rather than at it.

Your head should remain dead still from start to finish. Listen with your forward ear {Fig. 8 – 14}. Your body may slightly move on very long putts, but will be very quiet with any normal length.

When your stroke is complete, hold your finish position until the ball comes to rest or is at least well under way {Fig. 8 – 14}. No re-coil.

Fig. 8 – 18

Quite simply, it is back – through – stop and hold. 1 back – 2 through – stop and hold.

Once again, keep it simple, there is no need to over complicate a putting stroke or any swing for that matter. Simply choose a line, aim the face, and roll the ball. If it goes in, great; if not, LET IT GO! Take the pressure off. "It ain't nothing but a putt!"

ChiPitching: Chipping & Pitching

Like putting, short shots around the green do not require a lot of strength, flexibility, or athleticism, so essentially anyone can be effective in this area. Also, because of the smaller nature of the swings the technique can be a bit more generic and require less personalization. What these shots do require is a little understanding of some simple concepts that will give you an opportunity to let the club do the work and significantly improve your score.

If you are looking to make more putts, the easiest way to do so is to hit the ball closer to the hole. Think about this: you make more than twice as many putts from inside five feet of the hole than you do from five feet to ten feet. Simply put, if you chip and pitch the ball closer to the hole, you will make more putts, so getting good with your chipping and pitching will make a significant difference in your scoring ability. This doesn't mean that you do not need to learn more or work more on your putting, but regardless of the putting stroke you have, more putts will go in the closer you are to the hole.

I am a firm believer in simply learning one technique and using different clubs for different results and strongly disagree with manipulating a club in any way to change the trajectory of a shot. If you open the face of your most lofted club because you need a little more height than it will give you, ok to an extent, but if you need the opposite, absolutely, not. If you need more height and less roll, use more loft and if you need less height and more roll, use less loft. It's as simple as that.

I do not really put shots around the green into a chip or pitch category, but for what it is worth, my definition of a chip is a shot that rolls further than it flies and a pitch is a shot that flies further than it rolls. That the club selection fits into the chip or pitch category matters not to me. Most people relate hitting a chip to using a mid iron and a pitch to using some sort of wedge. There are situations that require the use of a sixty degree wedge and by definition are chips, because they run further than they fly. On the other hand (not my other hand :), there are times when a seven iron is used and by definition is a pitch when it flies further than it rolls.

For most standard greenside shots with a decent lie, a very simple motion will adequately take care of the job. The only aspect that will change is the length and speed of your swing and the club selection. I call this chipitching; using one technique and choosing different clubs to get different results. The technique is along the same idea as the swing presented in this book, just on a smaller scale with a little less wrist cock.

Allowing the golf clubs loft to do the work for you decreases the need for any extra moving parts or timing. You may be surprised at how far and high you can hit a sand or lob wedge swinging from hip height to hip height with minimal wrist cock {this does not mean stiff wristed, but firm wristed}. There are, of course times when more height and length are necessary, requiring more swing length for speed, but less than you may think. A simple motion with the correct club selection will handle most golf shots inside 30 yards of the green, unless your ball is sitting down in high grass, which we will cover later.

The first club to look for when around the green is your putter. Within reason…. if you can putt it, putt it. If putting is not the best option because of what is between your ball and the green, use the club that will land your ball safely on the green, five to fifteen feet or at least within the first third of the putting surface, and cause it to roll the rest of the distance to the hole {Diag. 9 -1} {Fig. 9 – 1}.

Fig. 9 – 1

There are many factors that will determine which club that is, so let's go over the ones I feel are most common.

- The lie of your ball will always determine what you are able to do and the first thing to take notice of. If you have a good lie, you will be able to make clean contact with the ball and control is no problem, so you can use a less lofted club. If, however, you are down in grass, you will need a club with more loft. From such a lie, the ball will spin less and run more because grass is between the club face and the ball. The added loft will help you cut through the grass, will help apply as much spin as possible, and give you a little more loft to help the ball land softer. If your lie is not too deep in the grass, the technique for your standard ChiPitching shot will work fine. If it is rather deep, follow the guidelines toward the end of this chapter for coming out of deep rough.
- Is the lie of the ball up hill or downhill? If it is uphill, you will need less loft to offset the added loft by the uphill lie. If it is down hill, you will need more loft to offset the loft taken away by the downhill lie. Either way, let the loft of the club do the work for you.
- Is the green itself up hill or downhill? If it is uphill, you will need less loft to help the ball roll up the hill. If it is down hill, you will need more loft to help the ball spin and land softer.
- Is the green hard and dry or soft and wet? If it is hard and dry, you will need more loft to help the ball land softer and spin more to combat the bounce and roll. If it is soft and wet, you will need less loft to help the ball move forward with less spin. If the green is not saturated, but the grass is wet, be aware that the ball may tend to skip when it initially hits the ground and "hydroplane", this may make the balls first bounce more of a skip and go a little further before it starts to roll.

- Is the grass on the green short or long? If it is short and fast, you will need more loft to help the ball spin and land softer. If it is longer, you will need less loft to help the ball roll.
- Are you playing down wind or into the wind? If you are down wind, you need more loft to help the ball spin and land softer. If you are into the wind, you need less loft to keep the ball lower and help it roll.
- These days there is less grain in greens than in times gone by, but there are still courses that have some. If you are playing into grain the grass will have a dull color and play slow, so you will need less loft to take off spin and help the ball roll. If, however, you are playing down grain, the grass will appear shiny and play very fast, so more loft would be necessary to help apply spin and help it stop.

There is no magic formula to learn for short game club selection, as each of these variables occurs in different degrees of severity. The variables can also be combined to create many different scenarios that may offset one another to a degree or make the situation extra fast or slow. Each golf course will have greens that react differently than the next and each course will be different in its' own right depending on the weather or time of day. Once you are efficient with technique, you will need to spend some time getting a feel for different situations. Through a little experience and practice you will do just fine at choosing the correct club.

One way to get an idea for the club loft needed is to visualize the necessary trajectory of a ball if you were to throw it underhanded to a landing area five to fifteen feet onto the green and make it roll the rest of the distance to the hole. You can try this in practice. The lower you have to throw the ball to get it to the hole the less loft you need and the higher you have to throw it to make it stop, the more loft you need.

Again, the rule of thumb I like to follow is to choose the club that will fly the ball safely onto the green and then make the ball roll the rest of the way to the hole {Fig. 9 -1 and Diag. 9 – 1}. The area five to fifteen feet on to the green is not a distance written in stone. It is only my recommended distance. You may like to fly the ball further into the green. I do not advocate that and would like to see the ball on the ground as soon as possible. Just be aware that the further into the green you fly the ball the more lofted club you will need to choose, the more difficult the shot, and the bigger your misses will be.

There are times that you may even need to fly the ball short of the green and use the fairway or fringe instead of a landing area on the green {Fig. 9 – 2}. Some instances possibly requiring that may be: having a less than desirable lie, having very little green to work with, hitting to a green higher than your ball, or trying to find a landing area that is flat. The better you are able to imagine and visualize each given shot, the broader your shot selection will become. The same principles apply; visualize where you would like to fly the ball, choose the club that will roll it the rest of the way to the hole, focus your eyes on the landing area, and then play the shot confidently.

Fig. 9 - 2

Now that you have the concept of chipitching and club selection, let's look at how to hit the shot. Below are the guidelines to a normal greenside shot with a respectable lie and within 50 yards or so depending on the player

Setup

- Grip approximately midway down the grip for more control. Also, grip slightly more vertical in your palm the shorter the shot {Fig. 9 – 3 and 4}.

Fig. 9 – 3   Fig. 9 - 4

A modified reverse overlapping putting grip works great. It is modified, because the grip is not up the lifeline of your left hand but still under the pad of it. Simply put your left hand index finger over your right hand fingers instead of overlapping with your right hand pinky finger or interlocking. This will move the ball a little closer to you and get the shaft of the club slightly more vertical. A swing path that will stay on the target line a little longer with fewer moving parts and less clubface rotation will be encouraged from this position.

The shorter shots do not require much speed, so the slightly more vertical grip is used to help simplify the motion. If you are totally uncomfortable with the reverse overlap putting grip, stay with your normal full swing grip and grip a little less in your fingers, but at least give it a try. The longer the shot and more swing you need, the more to your normal grip you go.

- The leading edge of the clubface should be "square" and form right angles with the target line.

- Narrow and slightly open your stance {turn your toes toward the target, 0 to 5 degrees}, your right foot should be slightly closed to the target line and your left foot slightly open to the target line {Fig. 9 – 5}. This will help stabilize your lower body in your backswing and help you move the club through with your right hip and leg in your forward swing.

- Your shoulders should be parallel to the target line and your arms falling comfortably and freely beneath them {Fig. 9 – 6}.

Fig. 9 – 5

Fig. 9 - 6

- The ball position should be where the bottom of your swing is. The bottom of your swing will come where your throat is relative to the alignment of your shoulders. If your shoulders are parallel left of the target line, simply dangle your club under your throat and there will be the bottom of your swing {Fig. 9 -7}. It is there that you would like to place your ball. Ideally, for me, this point will be about in the middle of your stance.

The middle of your stance is the middle of your heels, not toes! To see where the middle of your stance is, get into your starting position and where your ball position feels correct {Fig. 9 – 8}, keep your heels where they are and rotate your toes to point at the target line {Fig. 9 – 9}. You will see where your ball position is in reality. What looks like is in the middle {Fig. 9 – 8} is actually too far forward {Fig. 9 – 9}. You can put your weight where you would like, right left or middle, but the ball will need to be under your throat when your shoulders are parallel left. I personally think it is easier to play from the middle.

Fig. 9 – 7   Fig. 9 – 8   Fig. 9 - 9

Fig. 9 – 10   Fig 9 – 11   Fig. 9 - 12

Fig. 9 - 13   Fig. 9 - 14

The Swing

- Your arms and shoulders will blend and work together to swing the club away from the ball. Your lower body should be quiet, yet react to the length of swing. Movement in your wrists will be limited, but natural {Fig. 9 – 11}. There should be more natural wrist set the longer your arm swing is {Fig. 9 – 16}, but less is better than more in my opinion. This does not mean locked and stiff, yet reactive to length and natural.

- Your forward swing will mirror or be slightly longer in length than your back swing with an even and unhurried rhythm and tempo. Make sure to swing the club far enough back that there is no need to rush your swing forward, yet not so far back that you have to decelerate at impact to apply the correct effort for the length of shot at hand. You would like for your swing to be accelerating through the ball.

- Your hips, legs, and feet will be quiet in your back swing, but will be what moves the club through the ball. Swing back….then push your right hip to the target {Fig. 9 – 12, 13, 14, 17, and 18}. This will move your weight into your left leg which is where we would like your weight to be at impact. Your arms will swing through, have no fear. Move the club through the ball with your right hip and knee. As your swing increases in length, so should the amount of release from your right foot, knee, and hip in your forward swing. This will allow your hands to keep moving and stay in line with or slightly in front of the club head through impact {Fig. 9 – 12 and 17}.

- Make sure that the grip of the club and the head of the club move proportionately in the same direction back and through the ball. If the club head is moving to the right in the backswing, the grip should be moving to the right. When the club head is moving to the left and through the ball, the grip should also be moving left.

- Let the toe of the club flow to point up in the backswing {Fig. 9 – 11 and 16} and through the ball to up in the forward swing {toe up to toe up} {Fig. 9 – 14 and 18} for a normal trajectory.

- Hold your finish position. Make sure your weight is in your forward foot. Your left arm and the shaft of the club should create a relatively straight line.

- This shot can be used to fly the ball a good 30 to 50 yards with a wedge depending on the person playing the shot. The only difference in the shorter shots and longer shots is length of swing, natural wrist set and overall motion. The shorter the shot the smaller the motion, the longer the shot the larger, but the overall technique is the same. The following set of pictures is simply a longer shot that required more golf swing, yet as you see the technique is the same. {Fig. 9 – 15, 16, 17, and 18}

Fig. 9 – 15   Fig. 9 – 16

Fig. 9 – 17   Fig. 9 - 18

One last thought on chipitching and summary
Make sure you set up so that you can use the bottom and back edge of the
sole. Most people try to help the ball into the air by swinging up at the
ball. This puts the bottom of the swing too soon and causes inconsistent
fat and thin shots. To combat that, many people try to lean forward and
hit down on the ball. To a degree, this may help, but be careful to not
over do this thought. When you lean too far toward the target, move the
ball back too far, and hit down on the ball, you are creating a shovel out of
the club and making it dig. This requires a very precise strike and makes

distance control harder. It may help out of rough as we will cover in a moment, but on a clean lie can be very difficult and inconsistent.

Set up more level as described above and think "through" rather than "down" or "at" and let the bottom of the club help you. The clubface will make the ball go up if you are swinging through. If you need more height, use more loft and more swing. Just remember, the more loft and more swing you use, the bigger the misses become. Simplify your motion, let the club face do the work, and choose a less lofted club if circumstances allow. One technique, different lengths of swing and club selection and your short game will be more consistent day in and day out.

Tough Rough

There is a little different approach to hit a greenside shot out of the rough. You would like to once again take your normal full swing grip, but a little firmer to help you control twisting as the grass grabs the hozel of your club. The grip adjustment is so you can set your wrists more to swing a bit steeper into the ball and to get more power and speed.

When in higher grass, put the ball in the center of your stance and for severe rough maybe even slightly back of center. Move your weight to slightly favoring your forward foot {Fig. 9 – 19}. Contrary to a clean lie, you will now be using the leading edge of the sole a little more by putting yourself in position to swing a little steeper into the ball. With this set up and a bit more wrist cock for a steeper swing, you will minimize the amount of grass the club must go through and help it cut through what it does go through {Fig. 9 – 20 and 21}.

Once you have made a committed strike down and through the grass, hold off your finish by checking up your swing. It is a more aggressive hit and hold swing rather than one with a big follow through {Fig. 9 – 21}. You must make sure to commit to these shots and swing with a purpose. A timid swing that is indecisive will rarely get the job done.

Fig. 9 – 19   Fig. 9 – 20   Fig. 9 – 21

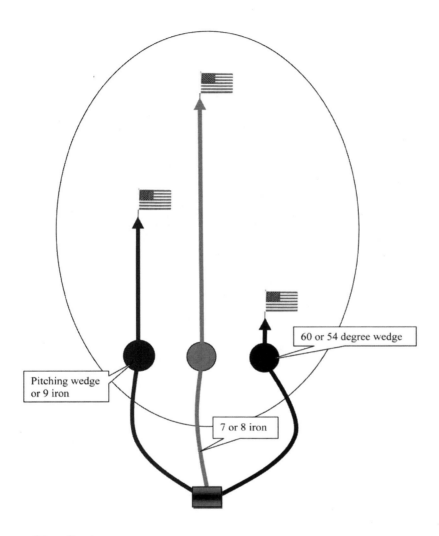

Pitching wedge
or 9 iron

60 or 54 degree wedge

7 or 8 iron

Diag. 9 – 1

Sand Bunkers :
Greenside & Fairway

Do you ever say, "oh no!" when your ball ends up in a sand bunker? Sand bunkers tend to strike fear into the average player, but are actually not that difficult to manage when a few basic thoughts are understood. Bunkers are hazards in the rules of golf, but in my opinion, they are not penal enough. A sand bunker should penalize an errant shot that finds one, but the way bunkers are maintained and raked they are simply not that difficult to play from. Some of you may be chuckling now because of the consistency of your local course bunker conditions and certainly because I said they were easy to play from.

I am a big fan of using rakes that have teeth set wide apart and long enough to leave a valley for the ball to settle down in {Fig. 10 – 1}.

Fig. 10 – 1

This makes a greenside bunker shot harder to control and a fairway bunker shot harder to make clean contact with. This would actually penalize an errant or greedy shot caught by a bunker by another ½ a shot. I do not think that will become the norm, so no worries. Most of you are probably saying, "bunkers are hard enough as they are! Leave 'em alone", "take them away instead!", but that's before you know a little more about how to think and play from them.

There a three basic sand bunker shots that we will go over. A normal lie in a greenside bunker, a buried lie in a greenside or fairway bunker, and a normal lie in a fairway bunker. A normal shot out of a greenside bunker and one out of a fairway bunker are two totally different golf shots. Playing from a greenside bunker your golf club should not touch the ball; the club strikes the sand first and the sand pushes the ball upward as you enter it behind the ball and "splash" it out {Fig. 10 – 2}. Contrarily, in a normal fairway bunker shot, the club strikes the ball first and very little sand is disturbed {Fig. 10 – 3}.

Fig. 10 - 2   Fig 10 - 3

We will first go over playing from a normal lie in a greenside bunker, then a buried lie, and finally a normal fairway bunker shot.

When the ball is lying nicely in a greenside bunker, we would like to use the "bounce" of the club to help it "skip/splash" through the sand. Bounce is the angle that the trailing bottom edge of the club is lower than the leading bottom edge of the club relative to a flat surface. The sandwedge {Fig. 10 – 4} has much more bounce than the 7 iron {Fig. 10 – 4a}.

Fig. 10 – 4   Fig. 10 – 4a

This angle {bounce} is what makes a "sand wedge" a sand wedge. The lowering of the trailing edge helps keep the club from "digging" and encourages it to "skip" through the sand when used properly.

You can relate to this concept by remembering a time when you put your hand out of a car window. If your hand was flat and parallel to the ground, your hand cut through the air. If you tilted the front side of your hand down it would dive and go down, but if you tilted the front of your hand up {like the leading edge of a sand wedge}, the air pushed your hand up. This is what the sand does to a club with bounce when swung through the sand properly. When you set up correctly and swing through the sand without trying to gouge the ball out, the club will skip through and the force of the sand will push the ball up and out of the bunker.

In short, a greenside bunker shot is no more than setting up slightly open to your target with a clubface square to your target and swinging through the sand under the ball with an accelerating motion. Sounds easy, it actually is. For a slightly more in depth approach, follow the guidelines below and have no fear. You will get out of bunkers more consistently. Once you are consistently splashing the ball out of the bunker and have the technique down, it's just a matter of fine tuning your distance control.

Setting up to the ball

Grip a little firmer than normal and down to the middle of the grip for more control. Point the "V's" between your thumbs and forefingers to your center {Fig. 10 – 5}. This will give you a slightly weaker grip than that of your normal full shots, which will allow you to use the bounce of the club a little more effectively.

Your ball position should be just left of center for a normal shot. If the sand is firm and/or shallow you might move the ball position more to your center so the bounce of the club is not quite as pronounced.

The leading edge of the clubface should form right angles {be square} with the target line. Square the face and point the shaft of the club in the general direction of your belt buckle. This will lean the shaft slightly away from the target if your ball position is left of center and will help you use the bounce of the club more effectively {Fig. 10 – 5}.

Your shoulders should be parallel to the target line and your arms hanging freely under them.

Your feet should be as wide as or slightly wider than your shoulders and slightly open to the target line with your weight evenly distributed right to left. Your right foot should be square to or slightly closed to the target line and your left slightly open {Fig. 10 – 5}. This slightly open stance and foot position will help your lower body remain quiet in your backswing and make getting to your forward leg and through the ball easier.

Your feet should be worked into the sand {Fig. 10 – 5} for 2 main reasons: 1) for stability and 2) to get a feel for the depth and texture of the sand. Playing by the rules of golf, you are not allowed to test the sand, but you are permitted to twist feet in for a firmer stance. As you are doing this, make a mental note of how the sand feels. Is it firm, soft, deep, shallow, crusty, etc.? If it is not consistent with your initial thoughts you will need to reevaluate and adjust the kind of shot you are prepared to play.

Your eyes should focus on the point in the sand the club should enter, which is typically, 1½ to 2 inches behind the ball depending on the texture of the sand: firmer sand closer to the ball; softer sand further away. This should not vary a great deal.

Fig. 10 – 5

Fig. 10 – 6

Fig. 10 – 7   Fig. 10 - 8

The Swing

Your shoulders and arms will swing the club back with very little, but natural and reactive activity in your hips, legs, and feet. There should not be a lot of weight moved in your back swing, but if necessary enough to allow for an adequate length of back swing {Fig. 10 – 6}.

The shaft of the club should be balanced between your arms and hands as your wrists cock up relative to the amount of back swing taken. I do not think there needs to be excessive wrist cock for a typical shot. Let your wrists cock up a normal amount relative to the length of swing {Fig. 10 – 6}.

Make sure you swing the club far enough back so there is no need to rush your forward swing in an effort of creating enough force and speed for the shot required.

Move the club through the sand with your right side. Just like any other shot, your right hip, knee, and foot are moving the club forward and into your left side {Fig. 10 – 7}. Accelerate through the sand. This does not mean to try and over power the sand and gouge out the ball, but to move through the sand with a purpose.

Hold the clubface slightly open, facing the sky after sand contact and through the ball {Fig. 10 – 7 and 8}. This is for a typical length bunker shot and will help the bounce of the club work more for you. You might even let your left wrist slightly "cup" up {Fig. 10 – 8}. This will shallow your swing through the ball and work the bounce of the club more.

A relatively simple way to control distance is to let the length of your follow through influence how far a normal bunker shot will go (assuming the correct amount of sand is taken). The shorter your follow through the shorter the ball flies {Fig. 10 – 9} and the longer your follow through {Fig. 10 – 10} the more acceleration and the further the ball flies. As with most golf shots, a little practice will go a long way here before testing it in competition. Your first objective is to consistently get the ball out and on the green. When that is the norm, controlling your distance is the next step.

Fig. 10 - 9   Fig. 10 – 10

The most important key for being consistently successful out of a greenside bunker is to swing through the sand to your finish and not at the ball and stop. It is not necessary to "throw" a large amount of sand out of the bunker. Think of it as a thump of the sand or a shallow splash, rather than a gouge.

A great way to practice normal bunker shots {obviously you cannot do this during play} is to draw two parallel lines in the sand about four inches apart and about two yards long in a practice bunker. Touch the middle of the two lines about every six inches with your club to simulate where a ball would be {Fig. 10 – 11}.

Fig. 10 – 11   Fig. 10 - 12

Starting at the beginning of the line, play a bunker shot with each mark you made between the lines. You will get immediate feedback for where you struck the sand relative to where a ball would be. I find that most people strike the sand too soon in an effort to help the ball out by swinging up at it or trying to gouge it out by hitting down at the ball {Fig. 10 – 12}. If that is your case....get to your forward leg sooner and get "through" the ball {Fig. 10 – 7, 8, and 13}

Fig. 10 – 13

The word "through" is key. Make sure you are swinging through the sand and getting all of your weight through to your forward leg. Your club will start entering the sand at the first line and exiting at the second {Fig. 10 – 13}.

Once you are able to consistently strike the sand at the first line, replace the marks in the sand with golf balls and make the same swing. If you are splashing through the sand, out your ball will fly. After a few series with the lines, play a few shots without them. You should be, at the very least consistently getting the ball out of the bunker. Now all that remains is to control the distance with your follow through. Be aware, that when you are varying the length of your forward swing, you must continue to swing through the sand and not at it. That word "through" sure keeps popping up doesn't it?

Buried Lies

The other shot you will encounter on occasions is when your ball is sitting down or is "buried". This will tend to happen more in a greenside bunker than in a fairway bunker and when the sand is deep or fluffy and not packed or settled. In wetter sand the ball will just go in the sand making a hole {Fig. 10 - 14}. In drier and fluffier sand the ball will make a crater similar to a meteor and is often referred to as "a fried egg" {Fig. 10 – 15}.

Fig. 10 - 14

Fig. 10 - 15

In both instances, controlling the ball is highly unlikely unless you are on an uphill slope and the trajectory of the slope helps you. There will be little if any spin applied to the ball; it will be a "knuckle ball", and will run when it hits the ground. There is an advantage to having a ball slightly buried when the hole is deep into green and/or uphill, because the ball will roll out to the hole, but when there is little green to work with, the shot is down hill, or the green is just plain hard and fast, you have to take your medicine and get the ball out to the best area to approach the hole on the next shot.

Sometimes in these situations, directly at the hole is not the best option. Look around and find where you can best approach the hole on your next shot rather than thinking that directly to it is the only way. It may very well be the correct line, but explore your options if a line to the hole looks risky. Remember, the ball will come out hot and run like a scalded cat. We'll call this shot just a good ole "chunk and run". Follow the guidelines above making the following adjustments to help you get the ball out.

Set up adjustments for a buried lie in a bunker:

- Grip the club even a little firmer. On a scale of 1 to 10, you may be at 7 or 8 now.
- Use your most lofted club and move the ball position back to the middle of your stance, if not slightly behind, keeping the clubface square to the target line. This will now lean the shaft slightly toward the target forming a straighter line with your forward arm and decreasing the bounce of the club so it will do more digging {Fig. 10 – 16}.

Fig. 10 – 16   Fig. 10 – 17   Fig. 10 - 18

Swing adjustments for a buried lie in a bunker:

- Cock your wrists up a little sooner in your backswing to encourage a little steeper and more powerful strike into and through the sand {Fig. 10 – 17}.
- You will need to swing a bit harder, because you are going to be moving more sand. Make sure to swing through the sand {Fig. 10 – 18}.
- Make sure your weight finishes in your forward foot through the ball. This is not an adjustment as we need to do this in a normal bunker shot as well, it is simply a point to stress. We are certainly not trying to "help" the ball out.

Fairway Bunkers

Again, in fairway bunkers the ball is struck first and very little sand is disturbed. Your normal full swing will be the base for these shots with a few minor adjustments to help you make that ball first contact consistently. Better players will tend to have fewer problems out of fairway bunkers because they already strike the ball first and their divots come after ball contact {Fig. 10 – 19}.

Fig. 10 - 19   Fig. 10 - 20

The average player however, tends to struggle out of fairway sand bunkers because their swing consistently bottoms out too soon; in other words, before the ball {Fig. 10 - 20}. When this happens either a fat shot or a thin shot results. It does not matter if the shot is from the fairway or a bunker, the result is basically the same. The only difference is that the flaw in the fairway bunker shot is magnified, because the sand is typically softer.

On the fairway or in light rough the ball will sit up a bit and create a little room for error. Especially if you play "winter rules" and fluff up your lie {not golf}. If you play by the rules of golf you must play the ball as it lies unless the rules allow otherwise. You will be a better player if you play the ball "down" and do not move it, because it will teach you to strike through the ball and will not let you get away with swinging up and at the ball as a "fluffed" up lie will allow. In the sand, however, even "winter rules" do not allow you move your ball and that margin of error grows. The slightest miss cue is magnified. A little behind the ball and "puff" goes your ball; a little thin and "zing" there it goes, into the lip of the bunker or too far.

Your normal swing will be the base for a fairway bunker shot. Make a few simple adjustments, pay attention to a few simple thoughts and fairway sand bunkers will become a little easier to play from.

Set Up

Grip down on the grip {Fig. 10 – 21}. As in any sand bunker, you are not allowed to ground your club, but you are allowed to firm and stabilize your stance by digging in your feet. When this is done you are changing your normal relationship with the ball because

your feet are now below the level of the ball and the club is above the level of the ball. Make sure to adjust for this by gripping down on the club enough to offset this change and to gain a little more control. Please do not adjust by pulling the club up with your arms or standing up. Gripping down on the club will help you maintain your normal posture and will give you more control of the club.

You will need to take an extra club to offset the loss of speed because of the grip down and the more in control swing you are going to make. Do not use too little loft at the expense of making sure you have enough loft to clear the lip of the bunker. After all, the main goal is to make sure that you get your ball back into play where you can get your ball in the hole in the fewest strokes possible without taking any uncalculated risks.

Fig. 10 – 21

Play your ball position slightly further back in your stance {Fig. 10 – 21}. This will make it a little easier to strike the ball first. Please do not over do this; too far back and you will tend to hack down or back out of the shot trying to help the ball up, neither of which is a good thing.

In your set up, I prefer that your weight distribution is as normal as possible, 50% left and 50% right. You may, however, try starting with a little more in your forward leg, maybe 55% left and 45% right.

Make sure your posture is up.

Make sure you have good solid footing by twisting your feet in. Consistent solid ball contact is highly unlikely if you are slipping {Fig. 10 – 21}.

Swing

Make a normal swing once you have made your set up adjustments. The set up adjustments will have made making ball first contact easier. Take one more club, swing shorter and smoother, keep your head up throughout the swing, and finish in balance with your weight in your forward leg. Finishing through the ball and in your forward leg is extremely important to me. Remember the loft of the clubface will get the ball up if you let it, so let it do its' work. It is typically better to catch the ball a little thin rather than fat. In other words, make sure to hit the ball first.

Bunkers really aren't that hard to play from. Make sure you understand the difference in a normal greenside bunker shot and a normal fairway bunker shot. Always swing through the ball, not at it, and commit to the shot you are playing.

Teaching Kids

CHAPTER

11

I have always enjoyed teaching kids and watching them grow both in life and their golf game. As a PGA Golf Professional, one of my {our} main responsibilities is to promote the game of golf to everyone, but especially to kids. They are the future of the game. Without a consistent effort to keep golf growing through kids, golf would eventually suffer and so would our profession. So, we all have a responsibility to golf and kids everywhere to spread the opportunity of falling in love with the greatest game of them all.

Parents, mentors, and PGA Professionals all play a role in introducing kids to the game and cultivating a love for it. Simply going to a range to hit some balls, playing putt putt, going to a tournament, watching a tournament on TV, or actually playing a few holes can prove pivotal in a childs' life. The life skills learned through golf will strongly influence a person for the better, especially a kid. Some of the qualities learned through golf and playing the game properly include, but are certainly not limited to respect, responsibility, patience, manners, honor, integrity, and perseverance. I think it is very important that we instill these qualities in our children and golf just happens to be the greatest activity of all to do so. Horses are good too Winona :)

Spending time with kids, friends, and family on a golf course are memories that will last a lifetime. Some of the most cherished times in my life have involved golf with my son and daughter; times that will remain in my soul forever {Fig. 11 – 1, 2, 3, and 4}.

Fig. 11 - 1

Fig. 11 – 2

Fig. 11 – 3

Fig. 11 – 4

I introduced my kids, Nickolas and Winona, to golf when they were old enough to hold a club and started developing their golf swings as soon as they could make a swing. The thoughts I worked on were very basic, but very patiently repetitive and consistent. These simple thoughts created a golf swing in my son by the age of thirteen that was one of the most technically sound swings I have ever seen. My daughters' swing was very good as well, but she was not quite as interested in golf. Maybe, one day that will change, but if not, it is ok, the seed was planted and she will always have a sound foundation to build on should she choose to play more consistently in her future.

The thoughts that follow are very simple and are what I teach kids until I see that they are ready to get more specific. If you can get a kid to consistently do the following suggestions, they will have a very solid foundation that can be built on by a local qualified PGA Professional. You may be surprised just how well the following thoughts work. Again, you must be patiently consistent reinforcing swing motions.

Attitude

I think keeping the game fun and uncomplicated is essential for all who play, but especially for a kid. If golf becomes work and/or boring, keeping a kids interest level up will be quite a challenge. I try to let kids be kids during cliniques and individual lessons as long they are respectful and try. Simply expressing good energy, high fives (high elbows :) and positive reinforcement has helped me keep the fun and excitement in many.

To me, there is no place for getting frustrated and/or ill with a kid that is trying, but having little success. He/she needs to be nurtured and encouraged after every swing that has an honest attempt. If, however, there is no honest attempt and/or their attitude is poor, we have a problem. I will not allow any kid to waste his/her time, their parent's money, my efforts, or distract a group if it is a Clinique.

A proper attitude is, to me, one of the most important ingredients to success. If a positive attitude is present, the chances of success are good. If one is not, it is my job to help create one, and then we are well on our way. I will first make sure I am making the lesson fun and challenging

{Fig. 11 – 5}. If that is not the problem, the kid has to understand that he/she will not continue until that attitude changes to a more positive one; period.

Fig. 11 – 5

Pre Shot Routine

Pre shot routines are a very important part of most successful golf games and should be introduced right from the beginning. It does not need to be an extravagant ritual, but get them in the process of starting from behind the ball, focusing on their target, walking in and aiming the clubface first, setting up to the clubface, focusing on the target, and then go. This process is for every golf shot, from the range, to each shot on the course, to the final putt. It may take a little encouraging and consistent reinforcement in the beginning, but it will soon become second nature and well worth the effort.

Set Up

As for set up and full swing technique, I follow a few basic thoughts and then let the kids' feel and hand eye coordination take over. My main goal is to consistently reinforce what should be done and encourage.

I always start working with any swing by first looking at the students grip. A golf swing will have a chance to react positively to a proper grip, but the swing of a negative grip will react with compensations.

The students' age and maturity will determine how exact I will get. For younger kids, I simply try to place their hands on the club with the correct hand low. The right hand for right handed players and the left for left. I do not worry too much about the connection {overlap or interlock}, only that their hands are together {ten fingers on the club}, the grip is more in their fingers than in their palm, the left hand thumb is slightly to the right side of grip center, and their right hand palm faces parallel left of the target line. The bigger their hands are or grow and the more mature they become I will get more precise explaining how their hands fit together and follow the model grip explained in this book. Once again, a good grip encourages a good swing.

For foot width I am mainly looking that their feet are hip to shoulder width. Typically a kid addresses the ball with pretty good foot position and posture, but if they are way off I will make sure they are in balance and look athletic with a straight spine and their head up. Posture is one the most overlooked aspects of a good set up, yet one of the most important to me.

Ball position and alignment are two more things that kids tend to do ok, but if they are way off, I will center the ball if they are using an iron {maybe slightly left of center}, if a wood/metal off the instep of the forward foot, and align them parallel left of the target {Fig. 11 – 6 and 7}. All of this said, usually the main real concern for me is their grip; again, they tend to do ok with the rest and too much information can simply be too confusing.

Fig. 11 - 6   Fig. 11 – 7

Full Swing Technique

When an acceptable setup is achieved, I will show kids how to cock their wrists up and down and do not move side to side. Standing in the address position and holding the club properly in their hands, have them cock their wrists up with their forward wrist flat until their arms and the club shaft make a ninety degree angle. Keeping the forward wrist flat will cock the club up at about a 45 degree angle to the side {Fig. 11 – 8a and b} and {Fig. 11 – 9a and b}

Fig. 11 – 8a

Fig. 11 – 8b

Fig. 11 - 9a   Fig. 11 – 9b

When they have that down, get them to turn their shoulders away from the target and swing the club up to their right shoulder with their wrists making the motion just rehearsed. The club should be balanced in their hands in front of their right shoulder {Fig. 11 – 10 and 11}. When the golf club is to their right their weight should be right. I will get them to pause for a moment so they can feel the club in balance and feel where their weight is.

When I say "simply swing the club up to their right shoulder with their wrists cocking up and balance the club", there are other things going on to check. One being, making sure they turn their shoulders to the right rather than just lifting the club. There could be much more talked about, but typically they will do a respectable job once shown a few times. The goal is to be as simple and uncomplicated as possible. Not unlike telling a kid to throw a ball and then demonstrating how, you do not go through the "mechanics" of how to throw the ball, you just demonstrate it and over time, they do it.

Fig. 11 - 10   **Fig. 11 - 11**

Once they can feel the balance of the club and their weight in their back foot, have them swing the club to their left shoulder in balance with their wrists doing the same thing in the follow through. When the club is up to their left shoulder all of their weight should be left and their right foot should have pushed in and up to their tip toe. Their foot should be vertical with the shoe laces facing the target {actually parallel left}. Once they get to their finish, in balance, they should be able to hold that position for a count of three {1, 2, 3} {Fig. 11 – 12 and 13}. As we are going through this, I will make a few easy swings so they can see what they should be trying to do and give them a motion to mimic.

Fig. 11 - 12   Fig. 11 - 13

So……. basically, there are just three points to check: set up, the top of
the back swing, and the end position. The motions and positions between

these three points will be relatively good if they start well, are at the top of the backswing in balance, and finish in balance. I simply say, "right shoulder, left shoulder, count 1-2-3". Sounds simple, is simple, just give it a try. There will be plenty of time for fine tuning.

Kids are amazing at how they mimic people they see swinging a golf club. I have seen kids that swing almost identical to a parent, both good and bad motions. If you are going to demonstrate, make sure your motion is respectable.

The kids swing may be a little rough around the edges but, the main points I am interested in is that their wrists cock properly, they can balance the club at the top of the backswing, can swing to a balanced finish position with their back foot pushed in and up to a vertical position with laces to the target, and can count 1-2-3. When they are consistent with this swinging motion and in balance, I will begin to fine tune their motion and get pickier with the specifics.

As the kid is making this golf swing, it is very important to me that the good things he/she is doing are stressed and their attention is taken away from the result of the golf shot, unless it is good :). Taking attention away from the result {if they are not great} may be easier said than done, but the golf shots will do just fine in time if they are making this motion.

Please, try to avoid telling kids to keep their left arm rigid and straight, keep their head dead still, and for sure not to keep their head down. Let them swing and create motion. Again, there will be plenty of time for fine tuning. As they get more efficient with the motion of a swing you can steady their head, create extension at the top of the swing, and so on. Keep the motion simple, uncomplicated, athletic, and balanced. Turn their shoulders, swing to the right shoulder, and balance the club. Push the right hip through and swing to the left shoulder, right foot vertical, balance the club, and count 1, 2, 3. Hitting a golf ball can truly be that simple, right shoulder, left shoulder, count 1,2,3.

Putting

Get them started making golf swings {that's more fun at that age....don't think that ever really changes :)} and then get them to a putting green. The putting green is where they will truly start to get a feel for a ball and a sense for the club face. It is also where we all get the true essence of the game; getting the ball in the hole. There are few successful professionals that can not remember the hours upon hours of time spent on a putting green alone practicing or with friends playing games. Most have challenged themselves to make a four foot putt to win The Ryder Cup, PGA Championship, The Masters, The US Open, or The British Open.

Putting is so simple yet can be made so difficult and complicated. There is truly little more to it than aiming the clubface on the correct line and rolling the ball with the correct speed. You may be thinking there is so much more to it than that or no it is not that easy, but yes it is. Watch a kid putt, there is no extra thinking about "how", they just do it with no fear. Sure they need to understand some simple guidelines, but all in all there just isn't that much going on in a putt.

Fig. 11 – 14

Once again, with anyone, but especially with children it is good to keep it simple. A great way to help a kid get an understanding is to set him/her up with their arms hanging comfortably under their shoulders {Fig. 11 – 14} and let them push the ball into a hole. Set the club head behind the ball and then push it to the target with no backswing. They will get a feel for the path of the club, where the clubface is aimed, and for accelerating through to a finish. One simple thing to pay close attention to is that their head does not move at all. Once they can move the ball in the correct direction with good speed, you can add in a backstroke.

As with the pre-shot routine with the full swing, get them to start from behind the ball, walk in and aim the putter face first, then set up to the putter face, and then go {refer to Pre-Shot Routing Chapter}. It really is as simple as aiming the face, setting up, keeping your head still, swinging one back, two through, and holding the finish position. If their speed is off and too hard, tell them shorter back and slower through. If too easy, further back and faster through. They will develop feel in their own time.

ChiPitching

Chipping and pitching are obviously a huge part of the game. As I explain in the short game chapter, I do not distinguish between the two, but call it chipitching. The technique in that chapter is what I would do with a kid as he/she advanced, but just starting out use these simple set up and swing suggestions.

Get them to grip down on the grip, narrow their stance, put a little more weight in their forward foot, and play the ball in the middle of their stance. For the swing, just match up the length of swing back and through swing; making sure that the grip of the club and the head of the club are moving in the same direction back and through. Encourage them to let their trailing foot release through the shot, and hold the finish position. Refer to the "ChiPitching" chapter as a reference. Try to get them to understand that the loft of the club will get the ball in the air if it is moved through the ball.

I think it is important for everyone to learn the simplicity of landing the ball in the "safe zone" and choosing the club that makes the ball roll the rest of the way to the hole. With that being said, I think it is also very important for people, especially kids, to use their imagination in golf. So, give them a seven iron, a putter, and a ball, and challenge them to play an eighteen hole short course. A short course is simply throwing a ball somewhere around a practice green within about twenty yards and playing to a specific hole from there. Do this eighteen times to simulate a round. Choose the seven iron first so they will learn to use slopes and because it is easy to hit solid. They will be forced to visualize where the ball must land and roll to get it close. Give them the putter so they will learn how to finish by holing their ball, and give them only one ball, because that is all you get in the game.

Change the club they are allowed to use from their seven iron down to their most lofted club, so they can learn the trajectory and spin that each club produces. Through this process, they will see which club produces the best results from different situations and all the while learning how to get the ball in the hole. Obviously, their objective is to complete the course in as few strokes as is possible.

Creating and playing games is a great way to keep practicing interesting, challenging, and fun. Games are not only good for kids, but adults as well.

100% on every shot

Again, attitude is, to me, the first ingredient to success in learning and playing. Playing golf with a positive attitude and trying your best on every shot is very important to me. Every stroke counts the same and deserves your best. At the end of the round, add them up and post your score. Make sure that that score is the very best you could have done on that given day. Anything less and you have let yourself down, your teammates down, your coach down, your school down, your parents down, and anyone else that is connected.

Equipment

A lot of great players got their start with a mixed match set of clubs and cut offs. Many a great player grew up with clubs ill fitted for them. While that is obviously better than nothing, the correct length, weight, and shaft flex is better. Finding the proper equipment for kids is now easier than ever. There are many companies that have seen the value of carrying a children's line that can be easily fit and fairly economical. It is much different than the old days when there were cut offs, ladies clubs, and then men's.

Try to supply your kids with a set as close as possible to the correct length, weight, and shaft flex. It is tough to keep up with growing kids because they grow so fast, but you can network a little and save some money by swapping sets with other parents in the same position. When your kid out grows a set, you may be able to recoup a little money by selling that set to another parent with a younger kid and buying a set from another parent that has an older kid that has outgrown his, and so on.

Parent involvement

It truly disturbs me to see how some parents try to live through their children in sports. Whether in golf, football, baseball, soccer, tennis, basketball, etc., etc. too often, parents go overboard in their expectations. I think a parents' roll is to introduce kids to sports, encourage them to do their best, and support them whether they excel or fail as long as they are giving their best effort.

Most parents will try to show their kids how to play a sport in their way. This, I think is fine to a point, but at a point the child should be turned over to a "teaching" professional. Unless the parent is a "teaching" professional in that given sport, it is in my opinion, better to let a proven professional or coach instill solid fundamentals that can be built upon as the child develops.

Whatever the sport, let the coach coach. Be positive and supportive. You do not always have to agree, but do not be critical of the child, the coach, or the team if there is one. Support them and look for the positive.

Introduce your kids to sports, but don't force them, let them enjoy them, and they will filter and migrate to the ones that they enjoy the most and excel in. Be supportive when the effort is there and tough when it is not.

Enjoy the time you have with them and participate with them. If you do not play, try it. If you do...... play with them. Do it now, they grow up awful fast.

Balance

Balance

Wow! What a word! It is a large word. Not in length but in scope. I think that balance applies to everything great and small. There must always be balance in what you do, whether it is in family, friends, relationships, body, work, fun, or life in general. There is always the search for the correct amount. Is there too much of this or not enough of that? And golf, oh yes, golf. There are many ways to apply the word balance to golf. Let's go over the ways I think are most important in no certain order.

How much time do you practice or play? Is there a correct amount for each? I think your goals and fundamental skills as a player will directly influence what is the correct amount for you. You must first determine what it is you would like to get out of golf. Would you like to play for fun or competitively? You should have fun competitively as well as fun with your friends, but there is a difference. To what level would you like to compete if competing is your desire? Just how good would you like to be? Would you like to win the weekend Nassau, your club championship, a city, state, or national amateur, or would you like to play professionally?

Depending on the level you have chosen to strive to reach, you must be prepared to commit the time and effort necessary to achieve your goals. If all you seek is to hang out with the boys or to play in the yearly company outing, I seriously doubt practicing with any level of commitment is a priority. However, if you would like to compete or it is your goal to be the best player you can be, you must have a plan and a level of commitment adequate to achieve your desired level. This requires balancing your time appropriately to cover all aspects of the game.

If competing is your goal, I think there is no substitute for playing, as long as you have an effective and repeating golf swing. By this I mean consistent control of your ball and sufficient distance. If this is true then playing and competing will only help you hone your scoring skills. This does not mean to exclude evolving/migrating your swing and practice to only play, but maybe play 60% of the time, practice your short game 25%, and your long game 15%. However, if you do not yet have an effective and repeatable golf swing, maybe you should flip those percentages and spend more time on the range {with a purpose} than playing.

Learning how to score through playing is a great thing, but if you are always scrambling to save par and bogey because you do not possess consistent control of your ball, you are simply not going to score consistently low. Therefore, working on building a sound, repeatable, and efficient golf swing that you understand would be my suggestion. Now you might practice 50% on the mechanics of your full swing, 25% on short game, and 25% playing. This may be the balance of the time you use until your ball striking is sound, at which time you should reevaluate and adjust accordingly to what needs the most attention. This process is always adapting to keep the proper balance of how and where you apply your time.

If just playing for fun is your goal, you must identify what having fun means to you. Do you define having fun as being outside and with friends, if so, play. You must remember though that the people that want to play with you may become more limited the worse you play.

Does playing respectably constitute having fun? Normally, the better one plays, the more fun one has. Whatever your definition is, you must allocate and balance your time realistically to maximize your fun. If playing better gives you more fun, you cannot expect to have a lot of fun if you do not balance your time and practice accordingly to maintain the level you desire.

If playing better is a goal, on what do you spend your time practicing? Is there a balance?

Typically, if you are practicing, you have a desire to compete, score your best, or at least score better; but how are you practicing? Are you the person that hits hundreds of balls, seldom devoting any time to short game, thinking the more balls you hit the lower your scores will go? You may improve your scores a little, but remember, even the best players in the world miss more shots than they hit perfectly. The difference is that those misses are very manageable and they are so good with their short game that they can recover and get the ball in the hole.

There is room for error the further away from the hole you are, both in distance and direction, but the closer you get to the hole, the more precise your distance and direction must be. The difference that separates the great player from the good player lies in the ability to get the ball in the hole. Never lose site of the ultimate goal in golf; hole your ball in the least amount of strokes possible. So, once you have a clue about your swing and where the ball is going, there needs to be a balance of time spent between practicing ball striking and short game.

If you have control of your ball and are sufficiently long, I would suggest that up to 70% of your practice time be spent on short game {chipping, pitching, putting, and bunkers}. If not, then maybe the other way around, until you do have some sort of control {you must be practicing mechanics that work and with purpose}. Please, do not misunderstand this segment to say that ball striking is not as important as short game, for I actually think ball striking to be more important, at least until a level of proficiency is reached. If you do not have control of your ball from tee to green, you can be as good as you would like with your short game, but getting up and down for bogeys and doubles will not get you very far.

Actually write down what you should be practicing during your practice sessions and allocate the appropriate percentage of time where necessary. These percentages will change depending on the state of your game. There should be a balance between playing and practicing and also a balance between what you are practicing. You can get a little more information on this in the "Tracking Your Game" and "How To Practice" chapters. Find the balance you need and watch your scores go down.

Balancing golf with life

This is a sticky one. I think it is fairly common that a conflict arises here with most everyone that plays golf. Whether it is with a relationship, children, other activities, or work, golf is simply time consuming, but for many is a way of life. It has caused many a strife between man and woman, man and work, and the other way around.

I have committed most of my life to the game. There was a time for the better part of 15 years that I might not miss 20 days a year playing or at least practicing. The other 20 years were not much different as golf was in some form a part of my day. I learned later in life to take time away, especially with my family. It is even a tougher balancing act when golf is your career since golf is quite often the topic of conversation when out for dinner, lunch, or basically any social function.

I certainly do not claim to know what the correct balance is for anyone, but do feel that it is very important to find some sort of balance between the game and life as best you can. You be the judge. Be fair and good luck. :)

Balancing your body during your swing

Balancing your body throughout your swing could be the single most important physical ingredient to a successful golf swing. There are many unique combinations of motions and positions in golf swings that have been successful throughout the history of golf, but none, that I can recall, that were out of balance. Footwork could be the most overlooked aspect of the golf swing. If your feet are not firmly grabbing the ground with the pressure of your weight in the middle of the correct foot at the correct time, you have very little chance of swinging a club with any kind of power, correct path, or consistency.

Try to remember a time when it was wet and one of your feet slipped. I would wager that that golf shot was less than desirable and the first thing you did after the shot was to look down at the ground where you slipped to put the blame on the ground. The ground is where you get power, leverage, and balance. Think of trying to hit a ball in street shoes off of a sheet of ice. Your chances of any significant blend of power, consistency, and control are slim, at best.

Balance problems come in golf swings when your weight moves out of the middle of the foot you are swinging around. This means your weight moves too far toward your toes, your heels, or the outsides of your feet. To maintain good balance throughout a swing your body must be properly stacked. Your upper body should be over your right hip and leg in your backswing {Fig. 12 – 1} and finish over your left hip and leg in your finish {Fig. 12 – 2).

Fig. 12 - 1   Fig. 12 - 2

I think that a golf swing is as simple as 1 – 2. That is, that you 1: turn back and then 2: push through. You turn your shoulders back against a braced back leg {1}, then you push your back hip through to the finish {2}. You should be able to hold both positions, in balance, with no trouble. When you turn your shoulders to the right your weight should be balanced in the middle of that foot {Fig. 12 – 1}. When you push your back hip through to the finish, your weight should be in the middle of that foot {slightly to the outside of this foot is ok}, {Fig. 12 – 2}. If you can do this you are well on your way to being a solid and consistent ball striker.

A great way to practice balance is to make some swings with your eyes closed. Awareness of your balance or lack thereof heightens immediately. Please make sure to do this in an open area and on grass just in case you lose your balance and stumble or fall. Try to do the 1 – 2 drill above; swing to the top of your back swing and hold that position for a moment {feel where your weight is in your trailing foot, it should be evenly distributed and coiled}, then push and swing through to your finish position and hold that position for a moment {again, feel where your weight is in your forward foot, there should be a balance and your trailing foot should be vertical with no pressure/it's not a kickstand}. You will become aware of if and where you are struggling with balance during your swing. Get to the point that you can swing in balance with your eyes closed and solid consistent golf shots will have a chance to follow.

Balancing the club during your swing

First, your body must be in balance to consistently balance the golf club. Balancing your golf club simplifies your swing and requires fewer compensating motions. A club is balanced when it feels light in your hands and arms at three key positions:
1} when the shaft is parallel to the ground in your backswing {Fig. 12 – 3}
2} when you are at the top of your back swing {Fig. 12 – 4} and, 3} when you are at the finish of your swing {Fig. 12 – 5}. At these points the club should not be pointing behind or in front of you too far, but should feel light and {for lack of a better word} balanced.

Fig. 12 – 3   Fig. 12 – 4   Fig. 12 - 5

A simple way to feel if or when your club is out of balance is to swing in very slow motion. Do so with a heavy club to make it even more obvious. From your starting position, turn back until the club shaft is parallel to the ground. If it is out of balance you will be able to feel the extra weight and see that the club is pointing too far to the right or left of being parallel to the target line. Continue to the top of your swing. Once again, you will feel if the club is out of position because it will feel extra heavy and point too far left or right of your target {this does not mean that you must swing to "parallel"}. Now, slowly swing to your finish and once again feel if the club feels extra heavy. Swing to the three positions mentioned above and move the club until it feels the lightest. When you find these points, your club will be "in balance".

The slower you swing the more obvious the position of your club becomes.

Heavy clubs are great to feel the balance of your club throughout your swing. If you do not have access to one, do so to the best of your ability with two clubs in your hands. This is not as good as a heavy club, but better than nothing. Even with the weight of one club in your hands, if you go slow enough, you should be able to feel the balance of your club or lack thereof.

Remember, anytime your club is out of balance a compensating motion must be made and the more compensations in your swing, the less consistent it will tend to be. Keep yourself and your club in balance to simplify your swing and gain consistency.

In summary

We can go on and on about this word and how it applies to so many things. The above mentioned are just a few that matter to me. You can think to yourself about how you can apply it to your game and life. Always look for balance in yourself, relationships, and of course... your golf game.

Tracking Your Game
What Should You Be Practicing?

How many people associate practicing with hitting a bag/basket of balls? Probably most. Most people are not really sure how to practice or, what is equally important, what to practice. We will talk about ideas on how to practice in another chapter, but let's find out some ideas on what to practice first.

Time is precious, so we should use it wisely. By using your time wisely I mean focusing on the area of your game that needs the most attention and with purpose. It may very well be your ball striking, so hitting balls on the range {with a purpose} may be what should be the priority at any given time. But, it may be your greenside bunker play that cost you an extra three shots your last round and two shots the round before. Maybe it was the speed of your long putts that caused you to three putt four times. As I am sure you know, there is much more to the game of golf than just wailing on a driver. So what should you be practicing and how much of your time should be given to that area?

Every student I work with gets a simple note book, pen, and a plastic zip lock bag to keep them in. I think these three items are a very important part of any players "equipment". This notebook is not only for taking notes on what they are learning throughout their Program and writing down questions they may have between lessons, but also for tracking their game.

Tracking your game takes only a few minutes at the end of a round to record. Doing so will give you vital information on where you should be spending your practice time based on your goals. By simply keeping track of a few basic statistics, you can see where you tend to lose strokes throughout a round. Once you create a trend and start to identify where you are losing those strokes, you can allocate percentages of your practice time to the specific areas of your game that may need more attention than just your ball striking. Your weak area may be that you are losing strokes because of lack of ball control, so the mechanics of your golf swing are what you need to be working on, but you cannot forget the rest of the game if you are going to be a complete player.

A few simple statistics to keep up with may be:

1. Fairways hit

2. Greens in regulation {1 shot to green on par 3's, 2 to par 4's, and 3 to par 5's}

3. Total numbers of approaches hit from inside 30 yards of the green

4. The number of those approaches hit inside the flagstick length

5. Total number of putts taken

6. Putts made inside of flagstick length

7. Percentage of greenside bunker shots hit to within flagstick length

8. Shots lost by lack of focus

9. Shots lost by lack of commitment

10. Shots lost by poor decisions

You can modify this list or add to it. They are just a few areas of my game that I like to monitor and encourage you to keep up with as well. The flagstick length is just easy to visualize instead of thinking in feet. After a few rounds, you will begin to see a pattern in each area. You may not be hitting your drives as far as you would like, but they are in play more than you were giving yourself credit for. A top 100 PGA touring professional averages less than twelve greens in regulation per round, so don't be so hard on yourself in that area. Just as another gauge, the average tour player is also going to make 60 to 70% of the putts he has inside of flagstick length.

The goal is to see where you are weakest and try to up the percentages through better thinking, better technique, and better fine tuning your feel and distance control. There is always room for improvement. No one will ever have 100% across the board, but you can try to even out your levels and become a balanced player. These statistics will also help you measure your improvement over time and give you a way to see how much you have improved. Not only will it help you evaluate your game and help gage improvement, but it is just plain fun too.

This day and age there are quite a few ways to track your game on the internet and even your phone. They will give you fancy graphs and percentages, for a modest fee and some are even free, that with an old fashioned notebook will be difficult and way too time consuming. I am old school and like the book, but suggest you may like to at least take a look at a few sites.

The following is a random example of how you might track your game in your note book and how to record your numbers to find your trends. I do not have a column for score or shots lost due poor focus, commitment, or decisions but strongly encourage you to keep track of them.

Golf Course and date	Fairways hit	Greens in regulation	Total # of approaches Hit / inside flagstick	Total # of putts	Putts missed inside flagstick	Greenside bunker shots hit/ inside flagstick
Augusta Nat 4/9/09	11	5	13 / 3	37	6	3 / 0
Pebble Beach 6/6/09	6	10	7 / 3	34	4	4 / 1
St. Andrews 7/14/09	10	12	6 / 2	30	2	2 / 1
Winged Foot 8/13/09	7	6	10 / 4	35	5	0 / 0
Oakmont 8/15/09	5	7	11 / 4	38	7	3 / 1
Pinehurst #2 9/9/09	11	8	12 / 3	37	4	2 / 0
Ocean Course 9/25/09	11	6	12 / 6	34	6	4 / 0
Valhalla 10/13/09	8	9	8 / 1	34	5	2 / 2
Averages	9	8	10 / 3	35	5	3 / 1

After a few rounds, you will start to see patterns of what this person needs to prioritize during practice. It looks like his driving is not so bad, his greens in regulation or approach shots are shaky but decent, but he is losing several strokes by not chipping closer. Simply put, the closer you chip the ball, the more putts you will make. Putting is not so good, especially inside the flagstick length and his bunker play is ok but nothing great. I would say this guy could spend more time on his putting inside the flagstick length and chipping. He could cut 3 to 5 strokes off his game relatively easily.

Keep in mind where the mistakes were influenced by lack of focus, commitment, or poor decisions. Your technique may or may not be the issue. The goal of tracking your game is to find out where you are losing strokes, but equally important is "why" you are losing strokes in that area. Is it technique or is it how you are thinking?

You can make your tracking as detailed as you like. Keeping some simple statistics about your game is a great way to measure your improvement, help you 'set goals, and help you prioritize your practice time. Spending an appropriate amount of time on the areas that are your weakest will help you become the most complete player possible. This does not mean you should neglect the other areas, but to spend a little less time practicing your strengths and more time on your weaknesses. Refer to the chapter on balance.

Spend a little extra time to track your game, practice where you most need to, and watch your scores go down!

How To Practice

The word {practice} as defined by Webster: to do or perform frequently, to form a habit of acting in any manner {can be positive or negative}.

Are you really practicing or just hitting balls?

When the average person "practices", 95% of that time is spent driving balls on the "driving" range aimlessly pounding "at" golf balls with little positive direction or purpose. Practicing is obviously an important ingredient to improvement, but if not done with a clear direction in an effective way, can and probably will be counterproductive, getting you little more than exercise.

I prefer to call a driving range a practice range, because "practice" implies a better message than "driving". A "driving" range, implies to me that you are doing just what I mentioned above, pounding at balls. Simply changing driving to practice sets a different image of what you are there for; hopefully to practice quality over quantity, which can be a great starting point to improving your game.

Most people that play golf actually do "practice" at least some. The problem is they do not practice with a consistent positive direction and purpose. When most people say they are going to practice, that practice typically consists of getting a basket of balls and hitting them. Yes, that is practicing, but practicing what. The definition says, "to form a habit of acting in any manner"; but what manner?

You can hit balls all day long, but if you are not doing so with a consistent positive direction and purpose {talk about repeating yourself, must be

173

important}, you are getting little more than exercise and more than likely engraining negative patterns.

First you try this, then you try that, then you try what your friend Moe says, then what Larry says, and don't forget Curlys' thoughts. It might not be quite that dramatic, but I am sure you have had days, if not most days, when it seems like there were at least that many opinions in your head from your own personal experiences, the many tips you have gotten from friends, articles you have read, and instruction you have seen on TV.

Choose and commit

Getting consistent proven direction is extremely important in my opinion, so that when you do practice, you practice with a positive purpose. No two Golf Professionals prioritize exactly alike. Some are similar in sequence of thought, but they will all convey their message differently.

If you were to ask the "top 50 Teachers" in America to analyze your golf swing, you would get 50 different approaches. Some would be similar, but there would be differences in what was emphasized, how thoughts were communicated, and/or the order of priority. This does not mean that one is right or wrong, just different. So, how in the "Wide World of Sports", are you, a magazine full of different authors, and your friends going to be able to create a consistent direction? Even the smallest of differences will affect the chain reaction of your golf swing and if one thought conflicts with another, more than likely, they will not match.

So; if you are going to learn from a book, do what that author says, and nothing else. If you are going to learn from a professional, do what that professional says, and nothing else. The point is; you must be consistent in your efforts, without contradiction. When you listen to anyone, including yourself, other than the source you have committed to, you are going to get mixed signals. This does not mean to not question or have your own opinion, but to be open to the direction you have chosen and give it a chance to come full circle. Remember PuzzleDuck. :)

Committing to learning from a single source is a big and sometimes difficult decision, but one that I feel is a vital part of making your practice time effective on your way to a better game. If you choose to use a source other than this book or me to learn from, practice using the guidelines set forth by that source. If there are no guidelines or you have chosen to use this book or me as your source, let the following thoughts help give you some direction on how best to use your practice time.

What if it feels weird?

Always remember, that if you do not feel different, you are not doing anything different, and therefore, nothing will change; "if you always do what you always did, you always get what you always got", Verne Hill. Obviously, you will hopefully get to a point that you will not feel anything different, because you have made the adjustments necessary enough through positive practice that they feel more natural. It's at that point that you would like to find a home and ingrain your motions through repetition so they become second nature.

The only things that will get in your way of succeeding {outside of physical limitations} is not understanding what you are trying to do and why, not committing to what you are trying to do, worrying about the immediate results of what the ball is doing, or trying something that will not work and doesn't match the other positions and motions of your swing.

Sometimes the adjustments will feel good immediately; sometimes it will take more time for them to feel comfortable. Sometimes, the results will be immediately better, but sometimes better results will take a little more time and a few more pieces of the puzzle. Stay committed and give it time. What feels weird will soon feel normal and what felt normal will hopefully soon feel weird.

With or without a golf ball

As far as I am concerned, in the beginning of making swing adjustments, the more practice you do without balls, the better {Fig. 14 – 1 and 2}.

Fig. 14 – 1   Fig. 14 - 2

When you practice without hitting golf balls your focus is on the swing adjustment and what you are feeling, not on the outcome of the shot, because there isn't one. When a ball is present it is human nature to get caught up in trying to "hit" the ball and the result. Especially if the shots are not immediately good, you will tend to compensate total commitment to the swing adjustment, which only slows down progress and gives you mixed signals about the validity of the adjustment you are trying to make.

During swing adjustments results are not always immediately positive. This can lead to frustration if you get caught up in ball results that are different than what you are accustomed to or are not good. This leads to tension and uncertainty, which leads to even poorer performance. Particularly in the early stages of swing adjustments try to grade yourself and how well you are making the adjustment rather than the flight of the golf ball. As you improve and fine tune your swing, reading the golf shot is very important, but not necessarily in the beginning of developing a more efficient swing.

If you are making good swing motions, your ball will show you good results. Your mind needs to be concentrating on what you are trying to do so it can remember what to tell your muscles to do and feel. It is difficult to stay focused on a swing adjustment if you are too concerned about what the ball is doing.

Positive and effective practice can be done right at home in your yard, garage, or even in your house {if your ceilings permit and you are doing drills in the air and not taking divots in the floor like I did one time many moons ago} {Fig. 14 – 2}. Your home offers a controlled environment so there is no reason you cannot get in a focused 15 minutes per day of practice. Staying in consistent contact with a club throughout the year will make a great difference in your comfort and familiarity with a club and your swing.

This does not mean that you should not practice with balls or that when you are it is not important to get feedback from the golf ball. Obviously, ultimately the resulting ball flight is the only thing that really matters, but not so much in the initial stages of making swing adjustments when all parts of your swing do not yet match.

Are you practicing or warming up?

It is fine to hit balls continuously when you are looking for rhythm or warming up for a round, but when doing so you would like to include your pre-shot routine every shot or at least as often as possible. The more often you do your routine with a purpose, the more comfortable and process oriented you will train yourself to be. It will also keep you from becoming a machine gun and just firing one ball after the next, which can destroy rhythm and confidence when you are not doing so well.

However, when making swing adjustments, I encourage students to use a five to two ratio: five drills or rehearsals to earn the right to hit two normal speed and length swings with a ball. I like this ratio, because it gives you a fair number of drills or rehearsals to feel the adjustment you are trying to make and then two full length, full speed swings to help you blend those adjustments and apply them to your full swing. If you just hit ball after ball at full speed trying to adjust your swing, making lasting adjustments is not likely and at the very least, difficult. It is simply hard to make an adjustment at full speed, even for the best of players.

Just watch the practice range at the beginning of the week of a professional tournament. You will see lots of rehearsals and drills {Fig. 14 – 3 and 4}. As the tournament begins you will see less and less of them, especially before the competition rounds, because the mindset changes to loosening up their body and finding some rhythm and confidence. After the round you may see more drills and rehearsals, but still not as many as in the beginning of the week during practice rounds.

Fig. 14 - 3   Fig. 14 - 4

The reason you see the change is that there is a difference between "practicing" and "warming" up. Practicing, is adjusting something in your swing through drills and rehearsals or once you have the motion you seek, engraining that motion so that it works subconsciously. The time for practicing is between tournaments and if necessary after rounds. Warming up, on the other hand, is just that, warming up. That means preparing mentally to play, getting your muscles loose, and finding your rhythm before a round.

Practice in a controlled environment
Always practice with a specific target; "aim small miss small" – Mel Gibson in The Patriot. Just in case I didn't mention this, always practice to a specific target. When doing so, use an alignment aid to help train your eyes to see and relate to the target with proper alignment. Improper alignment leads to a host of problems that will creep into your game and truly create havoc.

There are many ways to reinforce good alignment. The most common would be using golf clubs. Simply placing a club on the ground parallel to the target line between where your feet are placed and the target line. To do so, stand a few paces behind a club lying on the ground and hold another club vertical in front of your dominant eye. Line the club you are holding up with the one on the ground slightly to the left of the target so that it is parallel to the target line {Fig. 14 – 5}.

Fig. 14 – 5

You may also lay one perpendicular on that club to aide in ball position. Lay the grip on the shaft so that it does not move around so easily. I also like to stick tees in the ground on both sides and both ends of the shafts so they are not so easily moved through the course of practice {Fig. 14 – 6}.

Fig. 14 – 6

A really neat way to practice alignment is how my friend Ed Ibarguen has been preaching for years. He likes to use a 4 to 5 foot piece of florescent string. Tie each end to a tee and then stick the tees into the ground right on the target line. You can line it up using a club like described above. This is a great way to check your alignment, because you can hit right off the string on the target line. You also do not have to worry about it moving around {Fig. 14 – 7}.

I like to get students to practice setting up on a wooden deck parallel to the decking boards. There are lots of parallel lines to help you visually set up parallel to the target line and also to help you see the path of your swing. Although a golf swing never moves in a straight line, swinging along lines is visually very helpful for swinging to the target {Fig. 14 – 8}.

Fig. 14 – 7   Fig. 14 - 8

How much practice does it take?

So, how often do you need to practice to make a difference? Obviously, the more focused time you spend practicing, the sooner you will see results. I think it was Ben Hogan that once said, "Every day you do not practice is a day added to reaching your goal". That may not be exactly how he worded it, but the message is the same. I like to break it down even further and use minutes instead of days. For every minute you do not practice with focus it will take you at least an extra minute to achieve your goal. These statements are great motivators, for me, and are flat out true.

I ask my students to dedicate a minimum of 15 minutes of focused time per day to practicing with purpose without golf balls, which can be done right at home. Obviously, they are not limited to that time frame and are encouraged to do more with or without balls, but 15 minutes is a very reasonable request for any ones schedule. I prefer to see a student practice for a concentrated 15 minutes per day at home with no balls than go out and see how many balls can be hit in an hour. 15 minutes is no magic number and more time committed is more productive as long as that time is focused time with a clear purpose.

If practicing at home on drills, it is better to do so in shorter "bursts" than in a long drawn out session. In other words, doing two separate 15 minute practice sessions is better than practicing for a straight hour, loosing concentration, or getting bored and complacent with the drills. It is much easier to maintain focus in shorter concentrated time segments, than long drawn out ones that can be interrupted by external and internal distractions.

Turn the range into a course

Once you are finished with training the technique of your swing or to test what you are working on, put yourself into competitive and on course situations on the range. Actually play holes from tee to green. Visualize the tree lined fairway, the bunker, or the pond on the left. Use parts of the range like mounds, flag sticks, yardage markers, or trees in the distance as boundaries to define fairways, water, bunkers, etc. Go to the side of the range if it is lined by a boundary and use that to help you visually. The range could be lined by trees, a fence, or mounds and these can be used to help you create a mental picture of actual playing conditions.

Don't be satisfied if your ball just lands in the range itself. The range is a large area and just because your ball lands in it doesn't mean it would be in play. Where it lands on the range might be totally dead or out of play on the course. So try to create a virtual scenario in your mind so you can get some feedback and put yourself under some stress. This will help prepare you for actual situations on the course by making that tree lined fairway or shot to a guarded green less intimidating and will help you measure how accurate you truly are.

Reality Practice

There is always practicing at home and on the range, but {and this is at the risk of making every superintendent and golf professional in the world totally infuriated with me}, I think practice time on the course is very valuable. Obviously, this is done during very slow times and when absolutely no one is or could be behind you. This is also done with the utmost respect for the golf course, all divots, ball marks, bunkers, etc. must be repaired immaculately.

On course practicing puts you in more of a game situation. You can practice shots encountered during a round that are not the same practiced on a range or practice green. Even if you have an above average practice facility, it does not have the same feel as on course training.

If you can, go to a professional or high profile amateur tournament during the practice rounds and watch how they play a "practice round". The Masters is a great one to do this. A "practice round" is essentially what I am talking about doing. Getting a feel for the course, practicing shots you may encounter, creating a strategy, seeing how the greens react, and feeling the texture of the sand are just a few of the things you can achieve in a practice round.

This does not mean to take a shag bag to the course and wail away, but to take three or four balls and hit them from various points throughout the course that you may need practice or feel unsure. A few situations might be uphill, downhill, side hill lies, a tight tee shot, one that requires a layup, a tough chip or putt, or a bunker shot. There are numerous other instances and each person has his own weakness that needs attention {you can find that out in the Track Your Game Chapter}.

Practice rounds are not really for practicing swing mechanics, they are to get a feel for on course golf shots and situations. Sure….. you can think about and work on your technique, but try to stay away from getting too bogged down in swing mechanics. The place for that is on the practice range or at home. Make your time during a practice round help you become comfortable with the course and the shots you may encounter, to help ease any anxiety that may creep in due to uncertainty.

Summary

Practice with a purpose.

Fun & Challenging Games to Help You Improve

CHAPTER

15

Practicing does not have to always feel like work. In fact it is good to mix in some fun games to help your thought process, get more focused, enjoy competing against friends, and to keep you challenged. You can also measure your improvement in certain areas through games if you keep track of your performances over time. Games are fun and you can play them alone or against a friend or friends.

Putting Games

Let's start with putting. It is always easy to play putting games and it is after all, the game within the game. Putting games are fun and very productive if done with a purpose.

Have you ever considered yourself practicing when you take a few balls to the putting green and hit putts from hole to hole? Sure this is better than nothing, but not much, unless you are just trying to get a feel for the speed of the greens just before a round.

The next time you go out to the practice green to actually practice and are secure with your technique, play the games that follow to challenge you, to sharpen your ability to focus and have fun doing so. Even without working on your stroke technique you will improve, because you are learning to focus more and trying to simply get the ball into the hole. This doesn't mean that you do not need to work on the mechanics of your stroke, but the games themselves will help you with what you have.

My favorite putting drill is Drawback. Drawback is a very simple yet effective drill to help you with speed control and putts inside five feet. You can play this game by randomly selecting holes or set up a course in a particular order so you can challenge yourself multiple rounds or to compete against multiple opponents. Either way, after each putt that is not holed you must lay your putter down behind your ball and "draw back" your ball a putter length {Fig. 15 – 1, 2, and 3}. This is a great way to learn lag putting and focus you on the short putts, because a good putt left a foot from the hole now becomes a four footer that will test your nerves. If you can play 18 holes in even par {two putts per hole or thirty six} you are a pretty dang good putter. Of course, the severity of slope on the putting green and the distance between holes will make quite a difference, but even par is still pretty good regardless.

| Fig. 15 – 1 | Fig. 15 – 2 | Fig. 15 - 3 |

The next game I find useful is "Two ball worst ball". Again, you can do so on an outlined course or randomly selecting holes. Hit two putts to a hole. For each first putt you make you take off a half a stroke. If you make both first putts, the hole is complete and you score a "one". If you make one, you must continue from the "worst putt", but you take off a half a stroke. From that putt you continue hitting two putts from the worst putt until both balls are holed from the same place. This game really makes you concentrate, because if you make the first putt, you are still not in, you must make that putt again. You can make this game as hard as you like by adding another ball or even adding Drawback. Two ball worst ball drawback will really work on you.

One of the most fun games I have ever played is called "stymies". The more players in the game the more fun and laughs had by all, except the ones that get stymied.

Choose an order to start in any way you like. An easy and fair way is to have every player putt to the edge of the green and the closest goes first {a big advantage} and the furthest goes last {a big disadvantage}.

The rules of golf determining order of play from there. The first player chooses a hole and everyone putts. No one holes out or marks his ball. If you strike a ball, add one. Of course, if you are in you are in. The furthest from the hole plays from his first putt, but if another ball is hit, add a penalty stroke. The more balls in play the harder to avoid hitting another ball, therefore, positioning becomes a strategy. Playing first from the start is a great advantage.

Low score wins after 9 or 18 holes. You can play for whatever amount determined per stroke {can get expensive}. Many laughs are sure to be had at some ones expense. :)

Short Game Games

You can also play all three games from off the green. Playing them adding in shots from off of the green will really help you sharpen your whole short game. You can use all of the clubs in your bag or limit yourself to one plus your putter. I like to occasionally use only one club plus your putter because it will make you become more creative. Make sure that your greens superintendant is ok with pitching to the practice green before you do so.

There are many games that can be found or even made up to help keep practicing fun, challenging, and interesting. These are the three that I use the most for short game and have used them for many years. Be creative, invent your own, and challenge your friends to keep you focused and have fun.

On Course Games

On course games are also fun to play, provided you are playing them in very slow times and when no one is waiting on you. There are two very simple yet effective games that involve more than one ball.

The first is to, once again, play "two ball worst ball" from tee to hole. This is a very difficult game that will really make you concentrate and give you a good sense for where your weaknesses are. It will take you a while to complete nine holes, so nine holes is a good number to start with. If you really feel fresh, try it with three balls.

Another on course game that I like, I first heard Mr. Jack Nicklaus explain. He suggested to play three balls and play the "best" ball. He said that doing so will tell you what you are capable of shooting at your present level. I think it is a very interesting way to see just what you can do given three chances.

Summary

Try these games. Add to them, be creative and make up your own. Games are fun, can be done alone and can be done with friends. There is nothing like a little challenge against yourself or a friend to get the blood flowing and sharpen your skills.

Drills & What They Help   CHAPTER

Do drills really work? I think so. They are the primary medication that I give to students to help them feel a position or motion that will help their game. Five drills to earn the right to hit two golf balls. That sounds like work. It is work, it is working on your game. Hitting balls at full speed trying to make swing adjustments will seldom get the job done. To me, correct rehearsal of the proper position or motion at a speed that the adjustment can be felt and distinguished is the fastest and most effective way to improvement. This is where drills come into play. Drills guide you to feel the correct position or motion, isolate the feeling you are trying to achieve, and help you do so in a consistent manner.

I am not the greatest "training aide" fan {I do use a few}, because typically, the training aide does the work for you. Drill's, on the other hand, require you to be aware of the position or motion you are trying to achieve to do the drill properly. You can also do drills almost anywhere, at home, on the range, or on the course.

This is not to say that training aides are not effective, for I do like some, but I am simply more partial to old fashioned drills that can be done basically anywhere with no aide or at the most with a club. The drills that follow are the ones I use most in my daily teaching. There are many more.

Arms across your chest drill – Can be done anywhere

This drill is very simple, yet can sometimes be difficult the first time some people try it. It will help you feel how your body should move in a golf swing. Once you learn how, it truly is simple how your shoulders, torso, hips, legs, and feet should work in a golf swing.

To start, stand facing a mirror and place your left hand on your right shoulder and then cross your right hand over to your left shoulder. If you have access to a golf club, hold it across your shoulders the same way. Keep your elbows close into your sides throughout this drill. Now, take your foot position and posture. You should be balanced and athletic feeling. This position should be like your normal setup position, only that your arms are across your chest {Fig. 16 – 1}.

From this starting position, the motion of the backswing is a simple turn of your shoulders to the right, perpendicular to your spine angle {feel level}. Do nothing in your lower body, but allow it to follow and coil against your right leg. Your head can move slightly to the right, but should not go up, down, backwards, or forwards. Turn your shoulders as far as you can around/against a stable right leg maintaining the same right knee position you started, "screwing" your right leg and foot into the ground, and without losing your spine angle. The flexibility of your body will tell you when to stop. You should feel the coil of your upper body around/against a solid right foot, knee, and hip. Hold this position for a moment and feel that coil {Fig. 16 – 2}. Basically all of your weight should be in your right leg.

Now, simply push your right hip to the target, into and around a posted left leg, and to your finish position {Fig. 16 – 3}. Your right foot should be vertical on its toe and the laces of your shoe facing parallel left of your target {Fig. 16 – 4}. Starting your forward motion with your right foot, knee, and hip will be the correct sequence and you will notice that your shoulders will follow and unwind as a result. This does not mean to push your knee out to the ball, but to drive your right hip and knee to the target.

Quite simply, your shoulders load your back swing and your right foot, knee, and hip unload your forward swing. Your upper body turns your lower in the backswing and your lower body turns your upper body in the forward swing.

| Fig. 16 – 1 | Fig. 16 – 2 | Fig, 16 – 3 | Fig 16 - 4 |

Making swings with only your arms

This drill is a good way to help you feel the connection between the turning of your body, the movement and rotation of your forearms, and how your weight should move. It is fairly easy to feel and identify if a part of your body is out of harmony when no club is involved.

Outside of being a productive drill, a real positive is that it can be done anywhere and with nothing but yourself. Of course the one down fall to doing this drill in public is the many strange looks you may get. You may however get some great conversation started. Imagine how I look when I do it? :)

To do this drill, simply take your normal posture in setup with your arms hanging comfortably and your palms out flat {Fig. 16 – 5 and 5a}. Turn your shoulders back, swinging your arms to your right shoulder height with your palms and wrists flat at about a 45 degree angle to the ground {Fig. 16 – 6 and 6a}. Hold that position for a few seconds then push your right hip through {Fig. 16 – 7} to the finish, swinging your arms to your left shoulder. As your arms swing to your left shoulder let them rotate forward through the impact area {Fig. 16 – 7} so they are on the same 45 degree angle with your wrists and palms flat when you reach shoulder height in the through swing {Fig. 16 – 8 and 8a}. Make sure that you finish properly facing your target with your right foot vertical and the laces on that shoe facing your target. Make these swings and feel your weight, your body, and your arms move in harmony in your backswing and through swing.

Fig 16 – 5   Fig 16 – 6   Fig 16 – 7   Fig 16 – 8

| Fig. 16 – 5a | Fig. 16 – 6a | Fig. 16 – 8a |

You can also get a feeling and great feedback by taking a relatively large book and holding it with your left hand on the front cover flat and your right hand on the back cover with your palm flat or by putting your hands in a praying position {Fig. 16 – 9 and 9a}. Do the same thing as above and take note that when you turn to the right and the book is front of your right shoulder, it should be at about a 45 degree angle with the ground and parallel with the target line {Fig. 16 – 10 and 10a}. Push your right hip to the target shifting into your left leg and rotating the book through the impact area {Fig. 16 – 11}. When the book is in front of your left shoulder it should mirror the position in the top of the backswing {Fig. 16 – 12 and 12a}.

Fig. 16 – 9   Fig. 16 - 10   Fig. 16 – 11   Fig. 16 – 12

Fig. 16 – 9a   Fig. 16 – 10a   Fig. 16 – 12a

Grip down drill – With or without balls

This drill is one of my favorites. I have shown it to almost every student I have ever worked with for one reason or another. It helps rehearse so many good positions and motions and can be done right in your house or with a small modification on the range with balls. There are four main reasons I give this drill. First, it will give you a guide to swinging the club away from the ball in balance and on line. Second, it establishes the proper path/plane the club should be swung on. Third, it lets you feel how your wrists set or "cock" and fourth, it makes you feel how your arms should be releasing/rotating the club through impact.

Put a tee in the end of the grip and grip down on the club so your hands are on the very bottom of the grip, even slightly on the shaft. The club head should hover above the ground because you have gripped down and you should maintain proper posture {Fig. 16 – 13 and 13a}.

1   The first few feet away from the ball until the shaft of the club is parallel left of the target line and parallel to the ground the grip and tee should point under your left forearm. They should not be visible. Your shoulders arms and club should be moving away from the ball together {Fig. 16 – 14 and 14a}.

2   From the position above until your left arm is parallel to the ground in the back swing, your wrists should have cocked the club up such that the tee now points to the target line {as a guide, the shaft should be near a 45 degree angle to the ground}. Your hands should be in front of your right shoulder and your shoulders should have turned close to 90 degrees relative to the target line {Fig. 16 – 15 and 15a}.

3   To start the forward motion…push your back hip to the target. This will cause your arm to follow and swing from an inside path. As you are moving through the impact area, the club should be releasing by rotating forward to the left. The toe of the golf club should be rotating past the heel of the club. This is done by your

forearms, not your hands {your hands only hold the club and feel, nothing more}.

4   When your right arm is parallel to the ground in the forward swing the tee should again point to the target line {again it should be at approximately a 45 degree angle relative to the ground} with your wrists flat and your hands now in front of your left shoulder. Your wrists should have re-cocked the club up. At this point, your right hip should have pushed through so that your body is now turned to face parallel left of your target with no pressure in your right foot. The shoelaces of your right shoe should also be facing parallel left of your target {Fig. 16 – 16 and 16a}.

Fig. 16 – 13   Fig. 16 – 14   Fig. 16 – 15   Fig. 16 – 16

Fig. 16 – 13a   Fig. 16 – 14a Fig. 16 – 15a   Fig. 16 – 16a

Again, when the club is in front of your right shoulder in the backswing and your left shoulder in the forward swing it should be approximately on a forty five degree angle. This drill is great to help you see and feel the positions your swing should go through to produce an on plane and balanced swing with the proper release. Make sure that your feet, body, and arms are swinging in harmony and blending.

You can also do this drill hitting balls. Grip the club normally and use the tee in the end of the grip as your guide. Remember that this drill is only shoulder to shoulder and to be done at a comfortable speed so you do not need to really work at stopping the swing at shoulder height in your through swing.

Push a 12 Inch 2 by 4 away from the ball in your backswing – With balls

If you tend to swing the club away from the ball too fast, to pick it up, or without enough shoulder turn this drill is a great way to feel the club, your arms, and your shoulders moving together in the beginning of your backswing. This drill works best with a 12 inch piece of a 2 by 4 board, but can be done with most anything that will provide a little resistance and will slide away as it is pushed by the club. You can use a bottle of water or even use a golf ball.

Place the 2 by 4 approximately 10 inches behind the ball and just inside the target line with the short side facing the ball. Set up normally to the ball {Fig. 16 – 17 and 17a}. When you swing away, you would like to push, not hit, the board away. The club will leave the board as the natural arc of your swing rises above the board {Fig. 16 – 18}. The object is to keep the club moving away from the ball low and slow. You will feel your shoulders do the work. This feeling may feel a little weird initially, but you will make a better shoulder turn and a smoother more blended move away from the ball.

Fig. 16 – 17   Fig. 16 – 17a   Fig. 16 - 18

Forward hand on top of a club and swing under with trailing arm

If you tend to swing "over the top" and across the line from your shoulders and out of sequence, try this drill. It will help you feel sequence of motion forward and how your forward swing starts from your feet and not your head and shoulders. This will also help you feel a path back to the ball from the "inside".

Simply take your set up position, but place your forward hand on top of a vertical golf club from the ground {Fig. 16 – 19 and 19a}. Then make a few swinging motions such that your trailing arm swings under your forward arm. Make sure that your trailing arm is in a nice supportive position at the top of the back swing. {Fig. 16 – 20 and 20a}. Don't forget to let your back hip, leg, and foot start the motion forward so your arm will drop and move under your forward arm on the shaft {Fig. 16 – 21 and 21a}. If you do this drill with your shoulders first {like many} your arm will go too high.

Fig. 16 – 19   Fig. 16 – 20   Fig. 16 – 21

Fig. 16 – 19a   Fig. 16 – 20a   Fig. 16 – 21a

1 – 2 Static drill – With or without balls

This drill is another favorite of mine. It is very simple to do and really helps you become aware of your balance, position at the top of your back swing, and helps you feel a little clearer the sequence of what starts and moves your forward swing.

Take your normal setup, turn to the top of your backswing, and pause. You should be able to hold this position with no problem for an extended period of time and in balance. At this point you should be able to feel a loaded right leg {your weight should be evenly distributed throughout your right foot {maybe slightly inside} and your club balanced and supported just behind your right shoulder {Fig. 16 – 22}. If you, your club or both are out of balance, you should be able to feel that immediately.

Now swing to a complete finish, starting the sequence of the forward motion with your right foot, knee, and hip by pushing them toward your target into a posted left leg. At your finish hold that position in a comfortable balance for a count of 3 – 1, 2, 3 {Fig. 16 – 23}. You should have felt the sequence of your forward swing starting from your lower right quarter {your right foot, knee, and hip} and not from your upper right quarter {your right hand, arm, and shoulder}. It is important to know that your right foot, knee, and hip do not go toward the ball, but to your target. At your finish position, 100% of your weight should be in your left lower quarter {your left foot, knee, and hip}.

So, swing to the top of your swing and pause feeling your balance and the balance of your club. Then push to the left, swing through to your finish, and hold your finish position in balance for a count of 3 – 1, 2, 3. Think 1 – 2: one back to the top of your swing in balance and two through to the finish of your swing in balance.

Fig. 16 – 22   Fig. 16 – 23

Swinging on a deck – Without balls

Swinging on a deck will make you aware of the path of your swing and
help you correct it without any technical information, just natural reaction.
Set up parallel to the lines on the deck with the club head hovering just
above a line and simply make some swings (above the boards of course :)
{Fig. 16 – 24}. Take note of the path of the blur of your swing {Fig. 16 –
25}. At the bottom of your swing; is the blur crossing the lines from
inside to outside, outside to inside, or just touching the target line but not
crossing?

I like to improve the path of a swing first and then the timing of the release of the clubface. Ideally the club head path will not cross the target line, but touch it. If you are set up parallel to the lines, are swinging from your back shoulder to your forward shoulder, and not crossing the line the club head started on, you are well on your way to straighter more solid shots. Now all you have to do is time the release of the club face. The grip down drill will help you understand and feel that motion.

This drill does not answer the question, why is the club crossing the line if it is, but it will encourage you to react and reshape your swing according to the blur so the blur does not cross the line. Most people actually surprise me with how they reshape their swing path for the better, without thinking about the mechanics, but reacting to the line and the blur. This drill is not a cure all drill, but it will give you some good feedback and some different feelings in order for the blur to not cross the line.

Fig. 16 - 24   Fig. 16 - 25

Swinging up high and swinging from your knees – Without balls

Most people tend to swing too steeply down at the ball {have you heard that before?}. This in turn, makes releasing the club impractical. If you tend to hit pulls and pull slices you probably tend to swing too steeply into the ball.

Two great ways to feel how your shoulders should turn perpendicular to your spine and feel a shallower shaft plane, are to swing up high and to swing from your knees.

To swing up high, simply take your normal grip and set up. Then raise your arms until the club head is at knee height {Fig. 16 – 26}. From there make some full swings to a complete finish {Fig. 16 – 27, 28, and 29}. Make sure to use your legs and feet in this motion. You will feel a distinctly more around swing with a "flatter" shaft plane and also how your arms should rotate and release through impact. This is a great practice swing for on the course. My friend Brian McDaniel {RIP} used to use this as a practice swing as a junior. He was a player. Be careful not to whack someone standing behind you when you do this drill.

Fig. 16 – 26

Fig. 16 – 27

Fig. 16 – 28   Fig. 16 - 29

To feel the same feelings, but a little more exaggerated, simply place a towel on the ground and kneel on it {Fig. 16 – 30}. Make some easy swings from here being careful to not strain your back {Fig. 16 – 31, 32, and 33}. Most people will hack down into the ground quite a bit before where the ball would be. This is what you call, immediate feedback for a "steep" swing. Make a few more swings and you will begin to swing more around with the shaft on a much "flatter" plane and start to feel your arms rotating and releasing.

Fig. 16 - 30

Fig. 16 – 31

Fig. 16 – 32

Fig. 16 – 33

Swinging a Broom – Without balls

Yet another great way to feel a "more on plane" shaft angle. You can and probably will do this drill right at home. At the range, you would certainly get some strange looks :) Just get your ordinary broom out of the closet, set up with the straw vertical {Fig. 16 – 34}, and make some swings with it. At shoulder height in your backswing make sure the handle of the broom and the flat edge of the broom head are on about a 45 degree angle relative to the ground {Fig. 16 – 35}. Through the impact area, feel the broom rotating so that at shoulder height in front of your left shoulder, the broom is on the same angle and plane as in the backswing.{Fig. 16 – 36 and 37}. This is just like the grip down drill.

The long handle will help you feel a shallower more around swing and the resistance of the broom against the air will encourage you to use your legs and body to swing the broom through impact to a full finish. It's also quite the work out. Be careful not to let your significant other see you getting too comfortable with the broom in your hands or they may expect it more often and for a different reason. :)

Fig. 16 – 34   Fig. 16 - 35

Fig. 16 – 36   Fig. 16 - 37

Belt loop drill – With or without balls

Another favorite..... Be sure that you are strong enough to swing a club with only one arm before trying this. Please do not strain yourself. This drill will help you feel the proper sequence of motion in the forward swing and getting your right side through impact. I am yet to introduce it to someone that did not feel the proper sequence and drive of their right hip, knee, and foot through impact the way I feel it should take place.

Hold the club in your right hand only where your right hand is normally placed. You are going to have to use your imagination and visualize one in my "hand", work with me... :). Reach across your stomach and hold the belt loop over your right front pocket or just grab your pants or hip in your normal set up position {Fig. 16 – 38 and 38a}. Turn and set the club to your right shoulder the way you normally would. Make sure that your right elbow bends to ninety degrees to support the club {Fig. 16 – 39 and

39a}. To start the forward swing, give a little pull on the belt loop {not too hard, you do not want to break it or over do it, just feel the sequence} into and around your left leg {Fig. 16 – 40 and 40a}. Swing through with your right side to a complete finish, making sure to let your right elbow bend to a complete finish position {Fig. 16 – 41 and 42a}.

This sequence of motion forward will feel foreign to most, but is what I think the sequence and forward swing should feel like. Once you get a feel for the sequence and swing, do the drill with a golf ball. You may once again be surprised at what happens. If you do not hit good shots right off the bat, give it a little time and make sure to complete the swing whether you strike the ball well or not.

Fig 16 – 38

Fig. 16 – 39

Fig. 16 – 40

Fig. 16 - 41

Fig. 16 – 38a

Fig. 16 – 39a

Fig. 16 – 40a   Fig. 16 – 41a

Step drill – Without balls

This drill is to help you feel the sequence of motion in the transition to your forward swing. This sequence is the same as in any dynamic motion you have ever made. For instance, throwing a football or baseball, bowling, pitching horse shoes, skipping a stone on water, hitting a tennis ball, and the list can go on.

Most people tend to swing down at the ball with their arms and shoulders before their lower body engages in the swing. This causes a pivot around their right leg which moves their shoulders and arms outside of the proper swing path. For the club to fall and seek the proper swing path at maximum speed with the least amount of effort, I think the sequence of motion forward should start from the loaded right foot and leg at the top of the backswing. In other words, pushing your weight from a loaded back foot, leg, and hip into and around a posted and stable forward foot and leg is the sequence I encourage.

To help you feel this sequence of motion you need only pick up a golf ball and throw it underhanded or over handed as far as you can at a target. You will notice that the last part of you to move forward is your arm in the throwing motion.

To feel this doing the Step Drill, take your normal grip and set up position Fig. 16 – 42} and then put your feet together by moving your forward foot beside your trailing foot {Fig. 16 – 43}. Turn to the top of your swing {Fig. 16 – 44}, then, in a fluid and blended motion, step back to where your foot was, turn, and swing through to a balanced finish position {Fig. 16 – 45, 46, and 47}. The sequence is to step, turn, and then swing, most people will swing, step, and then turn. You should be able to immediately feel how uncoordinated and out of balance a swing then step feels. Do this drill slowly at first so you can feel the sequence. As you feel the proper sequence you can build speed.

Once you do the drill properly a few times, do it the reverse order again by swinging your arms forward and then stepping. You should clearly be able to feel a difference of coordination and balance.

| Fig. 16 – 42 | Fig. 16 – 43 | Fig. 16 - 44 |

| Fig. 16 – 45 | Fig. 16 – 46 | Fig. 16 – 47 |

Club throwing drill

Please be careful if you do this drill. It can be dangerous if you are not in an open field with plenty of room {especially behind you}. The looks you get will also be quite entertaining. Use older clubs that you do not need. This drill will help you feel sequence of motion to start your forward swing, path of swing, and extension through impact. Another great drill for the pull slicer.

Take your normal set up in an open area to a specific target Fig. 16 – 48}. Swing back and through throwing the club in the direction of your target {Fig. 16 – 49, 50, and 51}. Nine out ten people will initially throw the club left of the target. Some even straight behind them, so once again, make sure there is a clear area behind you and no one or nothing there. In order to throw the club in the direction of your target with any power and trajectory, you must start the sequence of motion forward with leg drive. Your right foot, knee, and hip must drive to the target first and the last thing to take place is the release of the club. Think to throw high and to the right.

Fig. 16 – 48   Fig. 16 – 49   Fig. 16 – 50   Fig. 16 - 51

| Fig. 16 – 50 | Fig. 16 - 51 |

This drill can be a lot of fun and give great feedback. I have had many laughs with students through the years doing this drill, but again you must be careful.

Split grip drill – Preferably without balls, but can be done with

With a good grip, the split grip drill is a "slice killer". I have actually had students play with this grip for short periods. It helps one feel how their forearms release the club face and square it through impact for solid contact. I cannot recall a time that this drill did not help a student feel actual solid contact with a ball and see the ball curve in a hooking pattern. Normally the student hits the ball dead left, but the feel of a solid strike and the sight of the ball flying further are very exciting.

If you hit slices and have trouble getting the club face to release through impact, simply take your normal grip {hopefully it is as we talked about earlier in the set up chapter} and then separate your hands two to three inches apart, and with the same relationship {Fig. 16 – 52}. Make a few swings without a ball first and feel what the separation encourages your arms to do. Your wrists will set nicely in your backswing and then rotate through impact {actually maybe a little more than we might like at first, as seen in Fig, 16 - 54}, both feelings you are probably not accustomed to {Fig. 16 – 53, 54, and 55}. When you feel ready, hit a few balls with your hands split. Initially, you may not make contact the greatest in the world, but give it a few tries. When you do hit one solid, your shots will probably go left {if you are right handed}, but you will also have a feeling of contact that you probably do not normally experience.

There is no rule in golf that says you cannot hold the club this way. So, if you are playing and struggling with a slice, hit a few shots with your hands split, get a feel for the release. I am not saying you should play this way at all times, but desperate times sometimes require desperate measures.

For practice, as with any other drill, hit five balls with your hands split and then try to repeat that feeling with your normal grip for the next two and so on.

Fig. 16 – 52   Fig. 16 - 53

Fig. 16 – 54   Fig. 16 - 55

One arm left arm swings – With or without balls

This one I can definitely demonstrate! :) Once again, the strength issue, please do not strain yourself. Most people tend to pull their arms through the ball instead of rotating them through the ball. In so doing this the clubface does not rotate and release soon enough leaving the clubface open at impact and restricting extension through the ball. To help feel the rotation of the club through impact and extension through the ball, make some swings with just your left arm.

Put a tee into the end of the grip. A white one is easiest to see. Grip the club with your left hand where you would normally and take your set up. With your right hand, hold your left arm (I'm not so good demonstrating this part :) just above your elbow and make some swings {Fig. 16 – 56}.

Try to make the tee point to the target line when your left hand is in front of your right shoulder in your backswing {Fig. 16 – 57} and then again through the impact area and by the time it reaches your left shoulder in the through swing {Fig. 16 – 58}.

Holding your left arm with your right hand will help your left elbow point down, which helps your forearm rotate the club through. Your left wrist should be flat. This is basically the Grip Down Drill with one hand and getting a little help for feel from your right. Both drills are great to feel release.

Fig. 16 – 56   Fig. 16 – 57   Fig. 15 - 58

One arm right arm swing – With or without balls

Again, make sure you are strong enough to swing with only one arm. This is another favorite drill of mine; very simple but very effective. This drill will help you feel getting your right side through the ball and into your left leg. It will also help you feel staying up and through the shot. If you do not stay up and get left, you will crash the club into the ground too soon. Not only will this not feel very pleasant, but it will give you immediate feedback.

Take the club into your right hand where your right hand would normally be positioned (I am not so good at showing this one.. :) Thanks to my student and friend US Army Special Forces Soldier Lance Jordan for lending a helping hand, pardon the pun :). Put your left arm behind your back and take a normal set up position {Fig. 16 – 59}. Make sure that your shoulders are parallel left of the target line; it is easy to let your shoulders creep open when gripping with your right hand only. From a good set up position, make a normal swing. The only difference is that you are doing so with only one arm. At the top of the backswing, make sure to support the club with your elbow bent to a ninety degree angle {Fig. 16 – 60}. From there, swing to a complete finish and again let your elbow bend at the end of the swing to support the club {Fig. 16 – 61}.

Fig. 16 – 59   Fig. 16 – 60   Fig. 16 - 61

Most people will initially hit fat shots and thin shots, because most tend to hang back on their right side; never fear. In time you will begin to stay up, get through the ball more effectively and start to hit some pretty good shots. Simply a great drill and feel.

Preset wrist and swing – With or without balls

This drill is very good to feel a solid position at the top of your swing with a proper wrist set and relationship to your body. If you tend to set your wrists too late and are a little sloppy at the top of your swing and transition, this is a good one for you. It will also help you feel a complete shoulder turn with your arms, hands, and club moving in harmony.

Take your normal set up position {Fig. 16 – 62a and b}. Then "cock"/"set" your wrist up in a way that keeps your left wrist flat {Fig. 16 – 63a and b}. This will be approximately a 45 degree angle from the ground. Keep your hands in the same locale, where they are at the start. Now....turn your shoulders until the shaft of the club is parallel to the ground and the target line {Fig. 16 – 64a and b}. From here...hit the shot,,,,, turn to the end of your backswing and go. You will feel a more solid position at the top of your swing, your shoulders, arms, and hands working together in harmony and simply "less going on".

Fig. 16 – 62a   Fig. 16 – 63a   Fig. 16 – 64a

Fig. 16 – 62b   Fig. 16 – 63b   Fig. 16 – 64b

Set, rotate, and swing – With or without balls

This drill will free up your swing and help you feel the release of the clubface through impact. Fig 16 – 69 actually shows too much rotation, but that is the feeling we are after. It is another great drill to help you ease your slice. A very simple drill and rarely have I not gotten the desired result I was looking for in a student.

Take your normal setup to a ball {Fig. 16 – 65}, cock your wrists up at approximately a 45 degree angle with a flat left wrist {Fig. 16 – 66}, and then rotate the club forward toward the target {with your forearms} so that it is parallel left of the target line {Fig. 16 – 67}. Be sure to keep your shoulders parallel left of the target line. From here, swing to the top of your swing {Fig. 16 – 68} and hit the shot {Fig. 16 – 69 and 70}. You will swing through the ball freer and with a more released clubface. As with many drills, it may take a few shots to get it correct, but you should feel a noticeable difference in how much softer your arms are and releasing through the impact area.

Fig. 16 – 65

Fig. 16 – 66

Fig. 16 – 67

Fig. 16 – 68

227

Fig. 16 – 69   Fig. 16 – 70

Step through drill – With or without balls

The step through drill is a great drill to help those that tend to "hang" back on their right side and not get through the ball. It will help you get into a better impact position and help you hit through the ball rather than at it or up on it.

Take your normal setup and make a normal swing. The only difference is that you are going to walk through the shot. Push your right hip through the impact area and take a step toward the target {Fig. 16 – 71, 72, 73, and 74}. If you have ever seen Gary Player or Chi Chi Rodriguez play, you have seen the step I am talking about. If you move out of sequence by starting with your upper body rather than your lower, you will lose your balance, hit it left, or not hit the ball solidly.

Fig. 16 – 71   Fig. 16 – 72   Fig. 16 – 73

Again, this drill will help you feel getting through the ball and help you hit more solid golf shots as it helps you feel staying up and getting through to your left side, rather than "hanging" back.

Fig. 16 - 74

Knock down shots – With balls

An all time favorite shot of mine during play and also a favorite drill; the knock down shot will help you feel and learn a good impact position and solid contact. The only way for a shot to be "knocked down" is for the shaft of the club to be leaning toward the target at impact. This is what will "de loft" the club and "squeeze" out the ball.

In order to get the shaft leaning toward the target at impact your body must also be in a position conducive to doing so. Most people do not have a swing that will allow them to initially hit a knock down shot, but by visualizing and trying to hit a ball as low as you can, you will begin to get closer to a solid impact position.

To set up to hit a knock down shot as a drill, take your normal grip gripping down an inch or two. You may move the ball position slightly back in your stance. Keep your weight distribution 50% left and 50% right {Fig. 16 – 75}.

The swing will be normal, except that you may swing a little shorter in your backswing and are stopping your through swing by the time you get to shoulder height after impact {Fig. 16 – 76, 77, and 78}. A key image is that you are committing to the shot and hitting through the ball, but holding off your finish just after impact, trying to hit the ball as low as you can.

Fig. 16 – 75   Fig. 16 – 76   Fig. 16 – 77

Fig. 16 - 78

I am not going to go too deep into the mechanics of this shot, only that you need to have your weight in your forward foot at impact to make this work {Fig. 16 – 61}. You must get your weight left and your right hip through the ball. It is NOT done with your shoulders.

Hit five shots holding off your finish trying to hit the balls as low as you can. Then hit two balls with a normal finish, but trying to get into the impact position you just experienced. It will be very difficult to hit the ball too low. Most people trying to hit the ball as low as they can will probably be just approaching a good normal impact position, which why even in play, hitting knock down shots is my favorite.

Impact position drill – Without balls

This is a great drill to do right at home or on the range. It will help you feel a powerful impact position and how to go about getting there or in other words, the sequence of motion in the forward swing. If done at home, lay a towel on the ground against something that will not move. This might be the base of a doorway or sofa leg. On the range or course you can use your bag, the wheel of a golf cart, or anything else that will not move easily.

Set up normally to the solid object you are going to push against {Fig. 16 – 79}. Once in a good starting position, push the club as hard as you can. Most people will do this with their shoulders, arms, and head leaning forward, twisting around no specific pivot point. This will be a weak effort compared to what we are now going to do.

Take your set up again, but this time, keep your head still and use your right foot, knee, and hip to push forward toward the target into a posted left leg. Your shoulders should remain parallel left of the target line and your head must remain still [Fig. 16 – 80}. The shift of weight will move your head forward, but it remains square to the ball and does not lead. When done correctly, you will notice a substantial difference in the amount of pressure you are able to apply to the object you are pushing on with less effort. To compare, go back to your setup position and push forward using only your arms and shoulders. The difference will be clear.

Repeat the motion going from set up to pushing into impact position as often as you like. You should become aware of just how much power you create through your feet and the proper sequence of motion forward.

Now try to feel the feelings you had during this drill hitting a golf shot. Repeat that feeling of sequence into a strong impact position with a ball and the closer you get to doing so, you will strike the ball more solidly with more of a penetrating ball flight, much like the knock down shot.

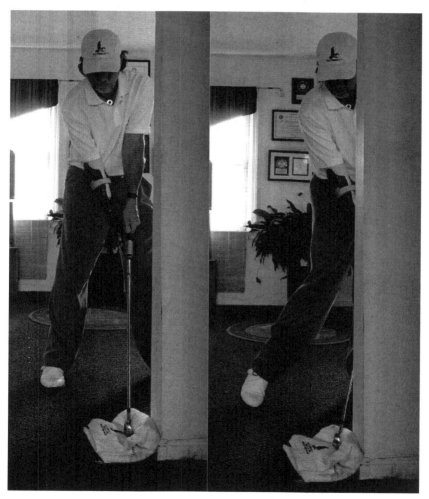

Fig. 16 – 79   Fig. 16 – 80

Weed whackin drill

If you tend to be inconsistent, hitting fat shots, thin shots, or high shots then whackin weeds is a great drill for you. Sounds like a commercial doesn't it? :)

Whakin weeds can be fun, especially when you are helping your feel for impact, but don't tell your spouse or parents that I gave you this drill unless you ask them first. This drill will really give you a good feel for striking through the ball in a good impact position and feeling the turf. It will also give you immediate feedback for where the bottom of your swing is relative to where the ball would be. If you are striking the ground too soon, you are not getting your weight into your left side soon enough. If you are striking the ground too late, your head is moving too far forward and probably out of sequence.

Weed whackin is done preferably in your own yard and again with the written permission from your spouse or parents :). So, here we go; find a weed in the yard and take your set up {Fig. 16 – 81}. Make your golf swing and try to strike through the weed, taking it up from the roots {Fig. 16 – 82}. Just clipping the top off will not get the job done. When you can consistently uproot the weeds, you are getting into a good impact position. Just a note….this is not hacking "down" at the weeds, but keep the words "thru" to your target in your mind! Now, apply this feeling to a ball and start making solid contact and quality golf shots. Have Fun!

Fig. 16 – 81   Fig. 16 – 82

Breathe in going back & out going through – With or without balls

Have you ever had someone try to get into your head by asking, "do you breathe in or out at impact?" Thinking about that can really derail your focus and cause big problems if you let it, but it can really help you with your rhythm and tension if you use this thought to your advantage.

If you tend to be tense, uptight, and quick in your swing, try to simply breathe in through your nose on your backswing and out through your mouth in your forward swing. Breathing in going back will get oxygen into your body and breathing out will help you relax through impact. Make sure that your breath is deep and unhurried. Focusing on your breathing can also help you simplify your thoughts. Breathe in deep and slow going back and blow out going through.

Breathing is obviously essential to life, but too often we do not breathe properly, especially in stressful situations. Try to become aware of your breathing. When you notice that you are breathing short and quick, take a moment and breathe in slowly and deeply through your nose and out slowly and completely through your mouth. Repeat this and feel your shoulders fall until you are more relaxed. Pretty simple stuff, but I think it's pretty dang powerful stuff.

Slow motion swings – With or without balls

Slow motion swings are a great way to feel what you are doing and what you are trying to do. It is very difficult to feel what is going on in a full speed full swing. Things are just happening too quickly, so make some practice swings at 30% of your highest effort level. Understanding your effort level in percentages and practicing at lower effort levels can be very beneficial in helping you become aware of what you are doing in your swing. It gives your brain a little more time to process the feel you are having. Look at the Effort Level Awareness Drill to help.

Super slow motion swings – Without balls

This is not as easy as it may sound. It can be difficult for many people to slow down their swing to super slow motion. Super slow motion means that it will take you a minute or more to make a swing. The slower you can go the more impressed I will be. Sounds easy, but….. give it a try. Super slow motion golf swings will help you rehearse swing adjustments, help you become aware of where your swing is, and help you feel your level of balance. You may just be surprised at what you find out. The slower you can do this the more in balance you must be and that is a good thing.

Towel Drill

The Towel Drill is a great drill to help you feel connection. It will help you feel how your feet and legs, core, and arms blend and work together. It will help you feel how your swing works from your inside out, not the outside in. If you swing your arms independently of your body, the towel will give you instant feedback.

Take a towel and put one end under your left arm and one under your right arm {Fig. 16 – 83}. Put only enough pressure in your under arms to hold the towel in place. You do not wish to get tense and squeeze the towel against your body. Set up normally and hit a few shots. Make swings only as high as your shoulders {Fig. 16 – 84 and 85}. If the towel falls out from under one or both arms at any point, you have instant feedback of disconnection. Again, you do not wish to squeeze the towel in place, but to simply have enough pressure to hold it in place. You will get a feeling of connection and unity between your arms and body. They will have to work in harmony to keep the towel in place.

This drill also helps you feel any tilting of your spine in a negative way which would make your elbows point sideways. The feeling is of everything blending and moving in harmony from one side to the other in balance with your elbows down. When your body blends together and your elbows stay "down" your arms and body will have a chance to properly release in an efficient and productive manor.

My first introduction to this feeling was by David Leadbetter. He used to use a thin rubber hose tied in a loop and push it down over your shoulders to just above your elbows. If you "disconnected" and let your elbows fly......that thing would pop up and whack you in the face....talk about instant feedback and a deterrent......It certainly made me think twice before I let my elbows fly! :)

Fig. 16 – 83   Fig. 16 – 84   Fig. 16 - 85

Swinging back & forth with no pause – With or without balls

Another favorite, yet very simple drill; this drill will help you feel how your legs, arms, and body move in the same direction and in harmony.

Take your normal set up and simply swing back and forth from your right shoulder to your left shoulder and back again, over and over without any pauses. There is no need to do this fast and hard, but steady and constant. Take notice of how your arms, torso, and weight in your feet move in the same direction. Your arms will not swing to the right as your hips turn to the left or vise versa. Feel how you blend to the right and then blend to the left. This is the kind of blending and harmony you would like to have in your normal swings. Add the step drill to enhance your sense of how your weight moves from right to left and how your arms blend with that motion.

You may also do this drill with balls. Line up ten balls in a row {you can tee them up if you like}. Begin with a practice swing, then without a pause, step to the first ball in line to make contact and so on through the line, again without pause, until you have completed the line {Fig. 16 - 86, 87, 88, and 89}. You may poorly hit many of the balls on your first attempt, but you must continue through the line with a consistent rhythmical pace and without pause. This is not a drill to see how fast you can hit the balls. Slow down.

Fig. 16 – 86

You will feel a flowing motion that is probably not a familiar one. You will also get winded, even at the slower even pace recommended. This drill can get expensive, because you go through balls very quickly, so use it at your own discretion. It is however, a very good drill to feel how your arms, body, and weight move in the same direction and in harmony when given the chance to react naturally.

Fig. 16 – 87   Fig. 16 – 88   Fig. 16 – 89

Swing Path Station

Feedback is obviously something we need to let us know what we are actually doing. Quite often you may "feel" like you are doing something correct, and may be doing better, but not quite as well as you should. A great way to get some true "immediate" feedback about your swing path is to set up a station. Swing path is what gives us the opportunity to release the club and after a solid set up position is established, is what I choose to influence first in a swing.

It is important to use something that will not hurt you if you should strike it during a swing. I wouldn't be doing this bricks. :) Use Styrofoam cups {set them up and put a ball in them if it is windy}, plastic bottles, or even golf balls. For added visual you can also add some shafts or dial rods. Be sure to give yourself plenty of room to swing safely, yet close enough to encourage a better path. You can set this up as easy or hard as you like. Start off favoring the easier and close them in the better you get.

To set up the station you must first establish your target line. The string is a great way to do this. Then set a cup, bottle, or ball just inside the target line on the target side of the ball and one just outside the target line behind the ball. Again, you can make this as hard or as easy as you like. {Fig. 16 – 90 thru 95}

For added visual and feel use the shafts or dial rods slightly wider apart, but in the same way and set them at about a 45 degree angle. {Fig. 16 – 90 thru 95}

Fig. 16 – 90

Fig. 16 – 91

Fig. 16 - 92

Your mind will react to the obstacles and encourage your body to make a better sequenced and more in to out or down the line swing path. This is typically the path that "most" are needing to get closer to, but for those that tend to approach the ball too far from the inside, it can be set up to help you as well. Just set the objects opposite from above. Put the target side obstacle slightly outside the target line and the one behind the ball slightly inside the target line. {Fig. 16 – 93. 94, 95}

Fig. 16 – 93

Fig. 16 – 94

Fig. 16 - 95

Effort Level Awareness

I am a big believer in being aware of your effort level. Few people are actually aware of how hard they are swinging. Most people are actually swinging at 90% when they are thinking 70, or 70 when thinking 50. The higher your effort level the more difficult it is to be consistent and the less likely you are to be in balance and/or strike the ball solidly. So when you are struggling to strike solid shots, are out of balance , or inconsistent......try slowing down to about 70 % of the effort you are capable of until you regain your balance and some consistency.

One way of understanding the percentage of effort you are using is to start by swinging at what you feel like is 10%, then go to 20, then 30 and so on. The idea is to be swinging at 100% of your effort on your tenth swing. Most people will be swinging as hard as they can long before they get to the tenth swing. Take your time and try until you can swing at 10 different effort levels and hit 100% on the 10th swing. A little easier way to start is just do 25, 50, 75, and 100% levels then try the 10% changes.

Most people swing harder and faster under pressure, when pressing for distance, and even when striking the ball well but wanting a little more. There is a point of diminishing returns. When you have awareness of your effort level, you can recognize when your efforts are starting to hit that "out of control" speed for you and slow down to get back into your peak performance range. It will be easier for you to stay in balance and strike solid golf shots more consistently by swinging "within" yourself and recognizing when you are not. 75 to 85% is typically an ideal effort level to strive for.

Swings with Eyes Closed

This is absolutely a great way to heighten your senses and ability to "feel" balance, sequences of motion, positioning of the club, and positioning of your body. When you close your eyes, all of your other senses automatically become sharper and more aware. Make slow swings at first to get comfortable with what is certain to be a little disconcerting at first. As you get more comfortable with the slower swings, slowly add a little speed. You will improve your balance and become more aware of your golf swing inside and out. Make sure to do this in an open area on turf, just in case you fall.

Visualization

This is more powerful than you may think. Seeing in your mind what you are trying to do is a very effective way to practice anywhere. You can do so before you fall asleep at night, on a work break, during practice, or while playing. Really anywhere, except while you are driving a car! :) Simply closing your eyes gently and visualizing what you are trying to do in your swing or seeing someone else that does what you are trying to do well will help you translate that into your own actions. There is nothing to get in the way of making the swings you desire if you clearly understand what you are trying to do. You can do ANYTHING in your mind and can do it anywhere.

In Summary

Drills can be very helpful when done properly and harmful when not, so take your time when you are doing them and make sure you are doing them correctly. They are also good to do to reinforce good feelings and motions even after you have made the adjustment. I like drills that can be done right at home and without balls so that you focus on the process and the motion you are seeking rather than the outcome of a shot. Remember, if you are hitting balls, try to do a ratio that will help you feel the adjustment and then blend that feeling into a normal shot. Five drills earn the right to hit two shots; a good rule to go by.

How to Take It to the Course

Have you ever said that your range game was not the same game you took to the course? Where did that person from the range go? Why is it that golf shots, seemingly, tend to go straighter, longer, and more consistently on the range? What is the difference? Actually, there are several factors that make your range game seem better than your on course game, but the good news is, there are ways to narrow the gap.

First; most people that do hit balls and practice do so with no specific target. Always practice with a specific target. If you do not, your perception of what you are actually doing could be skewed. If you have no specific target you have no way of gauging exactly what you are doing. The range is a big place, so an errant shot that is struck ok, may seem ok, but on the course could be in quite a bit of trouble.

On the course, the hazards, rough, trees, and out of bounds will let you know real fast if your shot is off line or poorly struck, but an open range without a specific target and bounds will not. So, once again, always have a specific target and boundaries so you can get some realistic feedback and know what to expect. The smaller and more specific you make your target the better your focus and more accurate the feedback.

Second; there are no consequences on the range, if your' shot goes astray you have a basket full of mulligan's right in front of you or if you are practice putting, you can just rake your ball back and hit the putt again. There is no pressure and when there is no pressure you will tend to get less stressed out over a bad shot or putt, because you can do it again without penalty.

On the golf course however, if you hit one sideways out of bounds or dump one in the water, it will cost you to complete the hole. This creates tension and uncertainty with negative thoughts which in turn creates less than desirable golf shots. Remember, to help manage this, use your pre shot routine and commitment to your decisions to help you relax, focus, and execute.

On the practice range, put yourself in competitive situations and actually play holes from tee to green or try to make a putt that matters. Visualize the tree lined fairway, the bunker, or the pond in front of the green by making boundaries in the range using flagsticks, yardage markers, mounds, or other distinguishable areas.

Try to create a virtual scenario in your mind so you can get feedback and put yourself under some stress. This will help prepare you for actual situations on the course and make that tree lined fairway or three foot putt less intimidating, because you have mentally already been there. While you are doing this, make sure you go through your pre shot routine to simulate game conditions. Not only will practicing in this manner help you prepare for on course situations, but it will also help your focus and give you that valuable feedback.

On the course, lighten up. It's just a golf shot. Do your best and then let it go. Good or bad. Every shot has its' own challenge, so try your best on each shot and then let it go. When you are on the range and hit a few sideways and then follow them with a few good ones, the ones that went sideways are more easily forgotten.

On the course, tension tends to build and snowball until the breaking point of when you finally "don't care", which puts you at ease and "Walla" you relax enough to hit a decent shot. Funny how that works. So why not skip all of the miserable feelings that accompany bad golf shots and just let them go from the start. You will play better. I will bet on that.

Third, on the range your lie is normally flat and sitting up nicely. The course, if you are playing by the rules of golf and playing the ball as it lies, is quite a different story. Your lie may be uphill, downhill, side hill, sitting down in rough, sitting down in an old divot, or just down on bare ground.

These scenarios are practiced by few people and provide a significant challenge, even to the best of players.

So why should someone expect to hit the ball as well on the course when they are accustomed to hitting off a perfect lie that is level? This is a big reason playing cannot be overlooked. Practice rounds help you encounter the many nuances of a round of golf and let you practice those that intimidate you the most.

As for the perfect lie most people get when they "fluff" up their lie {also called playing by winter rules}, you are only hurting yourself. My friend Bill Lytton has said, "if you are moving your ball to a better lie, you are not playing golf, but a version thereof". I cannot agree more. Playing the ball as it lies is how the game should be played and doing so will make you a better player. It will teach you to strike through the ball rather than letting you strike up at the ball. There is an advantage to teeing up your ball. If it were not, the rules of golf would allow you to do so more often than only in the teeing area.

However, if you are someone who must have help because of physical issues or for any other legitimate reason; before you quit the game, move it, or better yet, tee it up! Obviously, you will not be able to play competitively, but if you need help to get the ball in the air, use a tee, if it helps you have more fun and play the game more often.

I had a friend I gave a few lessons to named Morris Parham {most knew him as Papi} that played well into his 90's. One could always tell where he had played from because of the trail of tees he left. I got a chuckle every time I found one and thought it was great that he was out there playing and enjoying the game so late in life, even if he did use a tee from the fairway.

Forth, many people go straight to the first tee without properly warming up. This is an over looked reason for not taking your best game to the course. If you are going to practice you have quite a few balls to loosen up, find your rhythm, and no consequences, but if you are going to the first tee, it's game on from the first swing. If you are tight, in a hurry, and amped up you are not likely to get off to a very positive start.

Many people let the first few holes set the tone for their whole day. So, giving you a fair chance to get off to a positive start is very important.

If possible, try to get to the course an hour before playing. This will give you plenty of time to get organized, get a feel for the speed of the greens, loosen up, and find your rhythm.

You may not play the first few holes perfectly, but you at least give yourself the chance. I have always liked to get a feel for the greens first and then warm up my swing so I could go straight to the first tee without cooling down. The other way around and you have too much time between the range and the first tee.

If you do not have the luxury of getting to the course in time to go through a proper warm up session; stay calm and slow down. Always remember to breathe deeply and slowly. You have to be aware of your breathing to do this, so make a note to monitor it and your tension level. Try to hit a few drives if possible, the longer club will loosen you up faster. Wimpy Caldwell told me that when I was 13 years old. Ten balls in slow time is much better than twenty in a hurry. If you can, hit a few putts twenty to thirty feet long so you can get a feel for the speed of the greens. Over all though, just slow down and breathe.

Fifth, a round of golf is played over approximately a four hour period of time. There is a lot of "dead" time between shots. Finding a rhythm can be hard to do when you may wait five minutes or more to hit your next shot, let alone during a tournament or a slow Saturday or Sunday when you might wait even more. Throw in a few bad shots before the wait and you really have trouble.

On the range it is not so hard to find a rhythm when you have only a few seconds of "dead" time while you rake over your next ball. This is yet one more reason to practice with your pre shot routine and specific targets to make your practice time more realistic and productive. It will help you go in and out of focus so you can enjoy the time between shots and then re focus when it is your time to play.

In Summary

So….. how do you take it to the course from the range? Prepare better by practicing better. Practice your routine, practice to a specific target, practice visualizing, practice lies and slopes you may encounter, and practice committing. Give yourself time to warm up properly so you at least have a chance to start off positively. Be aware of your tension levels and breathing. Slow down. This does not mean to play slow. Play with a purpose, but slow yourself down. Use your routine to help you focus and commit. And finally, care, but don't care. Take each shot for what it is and let it go.

CHAPTER

Commit and give every shot your best

My best advice for managing a hole is to fully commit to each shot and do your best on each and every shot. A round of golf is just that, a round of golf. The round is not complete until the last putt is made on the eighteenth hole and the first shot of the round is equally as important as the last shot played. Shot 33 is a stroke just like shot 63 is, so commit and try your best on every single shot played from start to finish.

It doesn't matter if you are hitting your second shot on a hole or your seventh shot on a hole, you must commit and do your best. When the round is complete, add up your score and see what you have. You may be surprised at how many strokes you save by simply committing and doing your best on every shot. 88 is better than 90, 95 is better than 99, and 72 is better than 75.

This can be easier said than done, especially if you do not have the correct attitude and a solid pre shot routine. However, armed with the correct attitude and a solid pre shot routine, committing and doing your best on every shot is well within reach. You will score better, no doubt.

Greed

In golf the object is to start in a teeing area and hit the ball in the hole assigned to that teeing area in the fewest strokes possible. This sounds simple enough, but the architect and your greed have different plans for you.

They both try to influence you to try shots that are not practical, by enticing you to "go for glory", to get a rush by taking a chance, to catch your lack of respect for the course, lack of focus, and indecision.

It's not much unlike gambling in a casino. Human beings, by nature, typically are greedy. Greed "will" have its' way with you if you tempt it enough, in life and definitely in golf. The good news is, in golf, seldom will you lose your life savings with an ill advised shot {unless you are gambling for the ranch}.

The architect usually gives you a choice in the strategy you choose for a given golf shot. There is typically a way that minimizes the chances for a high number, but at the same time minimizes your chances for birdies and eagles. These choices that we must make each golf shot and the highs and lows that are associated with each outcome are some of what make golf so addictive to the typical person.

When you are on your game and confidence is high you can take a more direct line to the hole, but when you are off, it is wise to respect the course and play a bit more conservatively. Experience will usually educate in time as one goes through the ebbs and flows of being "on" and being "off".

With any decision in life or golf, there are consequences. There are degrees of success and failure, and very few second chances without penalty. We all make mistakes in life and golf. It is how we choose to manage these mistakes and how conservatively we chose that make us successful or fail. Since I am a golf professional, I am not qualified (that could be debatable by experience :) to get into the life aspect, let's go over how to minimize our mistakes in golf and manage each hole and round with greater efficiency.

Organizing your approach

Upon reaching the teeing area, begin to observe the best way to play that particular hole under the current circumstances. If the hole is visible, look from the hole back to the teeing area and see what length and approach angle will be the best to get as close as possible to the hole with the least amount of gamble. If it is not visible, go on experience, the card, or ask. Getting an idea of how best to approach the hole is beneficial, even if you do not have complete control of your ball. Just training yourself in the practice of thinking about a plan will help you manage your game better.

Try to keep your thoughts open to club selection by not immediately choosing your Driver or a shot that goes directly at the hole. Observe the lay out from the hole back to where you are and choose the club that will consistently put you in the best place possible to approach that given flagstick or lay up for that hole at that given moment. It may very well be your driver or a straight shot to the hole, but consider all of the options before making your choice. It may be better to hit the ball shorter off the tee so your ball will come to rest on level ground or to take trouble out of play such as a bunker, water hazard, rough, a tree, or out of bounds.

Quite often, it is better to hit a longer club into a green from the fairway than hitting from an awkward lie on a hill, the rough, trees, or a bunker after hitting a less than perfect driver. Many high scores culminate from simply choosing the wrong club off the tee and/or being indecisive. Indecisive swings seldom produce desirable golf shots and if you do not get the ball in good position from the tee it is very difficult to score consistently.

When on the teeing ground, tee your ball up; there is an advantage; if it were not you could tee up your ball anywhere on the course. It is also advantageous to tee your ball on the correct side of the teeing area. Look down the fairway and see where the potential trouble may be and where you would like to hit your ball. I like to tee my ball on the same side as any trouble may be. For instance if there is water on the left side of the hole, tee your ball on the left side of the teeing area so when you aim at the center or to the right side of the fairway, you will be hitting away from the trouble {Fig. 18 – 1 and 2}. This will hold true if there is out of bounds, a bunker, a tree, or any other trouble on that side of the hole. If the trouble is right, tee on the right side of the teeing area. If the trouble is on both sides, tee in the middle of the teeing area. After you choose your line of approach, make your club selection, tee your ball, commit, go through your pre shot routine, and execute.

Fig. 18 - 1

Fig. 18 - 2

Adapt your plan

Sometimes in golf, as in many things, we lose sight of the simplicity of the task at hand and over analyze and complicate situations much more than necessary. Just read any motivational book, there is no magic potion to help you; only logic and basic common sense. It's all about setting manageable and achievable {mini} goals with a plan directed at your ultimate goal.

Taking action consistently over time achieving the "mini" goals leads to achieving the ultimate goal. One of your mini goals is to commit and do your best on every shot. Another is to be flexible and adapt. Sometimes things do not go as well as planned and need to be adjusted, but the end ultimate goal remains; get the ball in the hole in the fewest number of strokes.

Once you have played from the teeing area, hopefully your ball has come to rest where you had planned or at least somewhat near where you had planned. If not, you may need to reevaluate your course of action. If you had planned to play from the right side of the fairway, but hit a pull to the left rough, your plan of attack may need to be altered because there is too much risk taking a direct line to the hole. As the Marines say, "adapt and overcome"; very powerful advice. Reevaluate the most logical approach to the hole location and once again, commit and execute. Repeat this process until your ball is holed.

Gamble if you must, but respect the averages and accept the consequences.

When your ball is in play, the first thing to consider is the lie. Will the lie of your ball allow you to execute the shot you would like to play? If not, what alternative will give you the best chance of holing your ball in the least amount of strokes, consistently?

As difficult as it may sometimes be, you must be humble in the game of golf or golf will take care of you being humble for you. Be honest with yourself, can you execute the shot you are thinking about at least eighty percent of the time? If not, think again about your course of action. You might get lucky and pull it off, but chances are, you are going to pay the Piper. Is the risk worth the reward? This is a very simple question, but a very powerful question! It may very well be worth the chance and consequences, but be prepared for the outcome {good or bad} and accept the fact that you had a choice and made a choice.

Learn from each decision you make. As you become more experienced, so will your decision making process. It is my experience that the more experience we attain, the more conservative we become. Kind of funny how this mirrors life in general for most, is it not?

Sometimes it is better to play wisely and aim away from the hole to an area that will give you the easiest and most consistent approach to the hole. This holds true when the hole is located close to trouble or any extreme edge of the green. Playing to the "fat" side of the green (the side with the most putting surface relative to the hole verses "short" siding yourself on the side with the least amount of putting surface relative to the hole) will give you a better chance of getting up and down should you be less than perfect on your approach shot. If you happen to error on the hole side of where you safely aimed, then a not so good shot, may turn out great.

You would also like to choose the area that is below the hole, especially when playing above average speed greens. Sometimes it is better to be off the green and/or further from the hole than in a position that is hard to control the speed of the ball, even if it is nearer to the hole. Once you have decided the best and highest percentage shot, it is once again time to commit, go through your routine, and execute.

If you have chosen to play away from the hole on an approach shot, make sure you are using your eyes properly by focusing on the target you have chosen. It is very easy to let your eyes wonder to the flag, but this will send mixed and confusing signals to your body. Your specific target may be the flag, but if it is not be sure to focus on what is..

Summary

Commit and do your best on each and every shot. Be realistic about what you can and cannot do. Make a plan for each hole and adapt it as is necessary. Play a little more conservatively when you are not on and a little more aggressively when you are. Know the difference.

Shots That Are Helpful To Have In Your Bag

CHAPTER

19

There are, of course, times in a round that you will face shots and situations requiring a little imagination and adjustment to your normal technique. Many awkward circumstances arise throughout a round of golf, so being able to adapt to the circumstances you are faced with is certainly an advantage. Knowing when and how much to challenge each situation will depend on your level of play, your experience and practice, your knowledge of how to play the shot, the circumstances, and your confidence. Here are a few of the most common and a few minor adjustments to help you when they arise. Practicing and preparing for each situation before trying in competition, will help with your confidence and level of expectation.

Long and uphill greenside bunker shots

Very few people walk into a greenside bunker with any other club than their "sand wedge" and most of the time that is probably the correct choice. However, there are times when opening your mind to choosing another club will give you better and more consistent results. When faced with a bunker shot that has a lot of green between you and the hole and/or is uphill, try taking a club with less loft. It could be from your gap wedge down to your 8 iron. I wouldn't really go any lower than your 8. The less loft will push the ball more forward to your target with less spin so your ball will "roll out" to the hole. You must, of course, use enough loft to clear the lip of the bunker.

Using less loft is easier and more consistent than making a huge fast swing to cover the distance with the loft of a typical sand wedge or "de-lofting" the sand wedge. De-lofting has never made sense to me anywhere. Just take a less lofted club and play normal.

Simply play the shot like your normal bunker shot, but with a less lofted club down to an 8 iron. Refer to the Greenside Sand Bunker Chapter for playing a shot out of a greenside bunker. Regardless of the club in use you are not trying to "chip" the ball out. It is a bunker shot and should be played as a normal bunker shot. The loft of the club will take care of the rest. Again; try this in practice before you do when it really counts.

Buried lie, uphill in sand bunker

Once playing Pinehurst #2 with Willis Denmark {RIP}, I had an uphill buried lie on the 17th hole with about 40 feet of green between me and the pin. I proceed to step in the bunker with my sand wedge and blast away. The ball comes out, straight up in the air, lands on the green, and because of the trajectory of the uphill slope and the sand wedge, rolled very little. So….. I had about 30 feet left. Willis says "I will do better than that with my putter". Of course, knowing the lie and my age {23}, I said, "yeah, right". "20 bucks", he says. I say, "show me". That was the wrong answer, but a great lesson. Relatively speaking, it was a rather reasonable price for the knowledge gained. :) First, I learned, you never bet a man {or woman for that matter} that says they'll bet you they can do something. Chances are….they can. Second, I learned a very useful shot that lead to opening my mind to using different clubs out of sand bunkers, rather than always going straight for my sand wedge. I had never considered otherwise before that.

Back to the shot, Willis recreates the lie {plugged uphill}, sets up comfortably with his putter, knowing he is getting ready to win an easy 20, and splashes into the sand. The slope of the hill makes the ball clear the lip of the bunker and the steepness of the putter pushes it forward. The ball lands with forward momentum, no spin, and rolls to three feet. He smiles {I call it a _ _ _ _ eating grin, oops}. I step in, recreate the lie, set up knowing I just lost 20 that I did not have to lose, and again take a big hack with my sand wedge. The ball, once again, plops out, lands with a steep decent, and rolls very little, again about 30 feet left to the hole.

Of course then I had to try it Willis's way. I recreate the lie, set up, this time with my putter and a sense of interest in the outcome, and splash into the sand. The ball pops out, more forward than before, hits the ground and proceeds to roll out toward the hole to about ten feet. I say to myself, "wow, I never would have considered that".

A couple of things to keep in mind with this shot are that the ball must be plugged in the sand, on an uphill slope, with plenty of room for the ball to roll. I would also not use my putter this day and age. Back then putters might cost $30 and the face was steel. Now they are much more expensive and made of different materials that can be damaged by the sand. Just use a five iron to serve the same purpose.

To play the shot set up as normal as possible for a greenside sand bunker shot. Because the ball is buried, swing into the sand with quite a bit of force. It will pop out as a knuckle ball and off it will go. It's not like you will encounter this shot very often, but it is a great one to have in your bag when you do. Your playing partners will think you are crazy when you go into the bunker to play a plugged lie with a 5 iron, but will think you are a genius when they see the result. I got several crazy looks when I went into the bunker with my putter back then. As always, try it a few times before you do so in competition.

Uphill, downhill, side hill lies

Not always during the course of a round are we playing from a nice flat lie. Some courses are flatter than others, but most have at least some slope at some point.

When faced with a lie that is on an uphill or downhill slope, my advice is to cooperate with Mother Nature. This means to swing along her rather than into her. To do this, simply adjust your shoulders so they are as parallel to the ground as you can get them. This will put your weight where it should be and give you the chance to swing along the slope.

If your lie is downhill, move the ball back in your stance an amount relative to the degree of slope {the steeper the slope, the further back to your back foot} {Fig. 19 – 1}. Getting through the ball will be easy, but getting back more difficult. Stay relatively steady with your head, there will be little movement of weight in your backswing. Swing smoothly along the slope. {Fig. 19 – 1a, b, and c} Take a little more lofted club relative to the slope, but let the club do the work {no lifting/helping the ball up}. Keep in mind that the ball will "tend" to push out away from you. These adjustments and thoughts are for shots around the green as well as longer shots.

Fig. 19 – 1   Fig. 19 – 1a   Fig. 19 – 1b   Fig. 19 – 1c

If your lie is uphill, move the ball up in your stance an amount relative to the degree of slope {the steeper the slope, the further forward to your forward foot} {Fig. 19 – 2}. Now, getting through the ball will be more difficult, but getting back easier. You will need to make a little extra effort to make sure you get "thru" the ball. Take a little less lofted club relative to the steepness of the slope. Keep in mind that you will tend to pull shots on uphill lies, because it is harder to get "thru" the ball. These adjustments and thoughts are also important to remember around the green.

Fig. 19 – 2

If the ball is above your feet, move the ball slightly back in your stance and grip down on the grip relative to the amount above your feet it is {Fig. 19 – 3 and 3a}. A tendency will be to move away from the slope/ball in your backswing, so be sure to stay steady and make a normal swing. The ball will tend to go left relative to the amount of slope, so you may wish to aim to accommodate the pull.

Fig. 19 – 3   Fig. 19 – 3a

If the ball is below your feet, again, slightly move the ball back in your stance. Slightly widen your stance a relative amount to lower your center {Fig. 19 – 4 and 4a}. You may wish to use an extra club and swing smoother to help ensure good contact and balance. The tendency here will be to move toward the ball, so be sure to stay steady and swing as normal as possible. The ball will tend to go right when it is below your feet, but be aware that when it is below your feet there is a chance that the heel of your club will dig into the ground causing the face of your club to flip shut, giving you the opposite of what you expect. Grip a little firmer to help you control the face in the event that happens.

Fig. 19 – 4   Fig. 19 – 4a

Wind

I absolutely love playing in the wind. This is the element that really lets you know if you are in control of your ball and striking it solidly. I am a big believer in knockdown/three quarter shots in normal play, but especially in the wind.

Playing down wind is always fun. "Tee it high and let it fly" is the feeling most associated when downwind from the tee. Playing shots into greens downwind is a little tougher, because the ball holds less spin and is harder to stop, therefore harder to control. Keep this in mind and try to allow for the extra run out. I recommend a solid knockdown shot downwind as well as into the wind, because it holds more spin and the wind does not affect a lower penetrating ball flight as much as a higher softer shot.

265

Wind from either side {right to left or left to right} is more challenging, but will affect the ball less the more solidly struck and penetrating the flight. A solidly struck "knockdown shot" will be affected less than you think even in strong wind. See the knockdown shot in the Drills Chapter. You can play side wind in one of two ways, 1} aim the amount left or right necessary to allow for drift or 2} bend the ball into the wind to hold it off. Your skill level, feel at the moment, and the circumstances will determine which is best for the given shot at the given time. It is easier to aim and let the wind move the ball for you, but you will have less control of the ball when it strikes the ground. It is more difficult to bend the ball into the wind the correct amount, but the more control you have in bending your ball flight into the wind, the more control you will have with your ball when it strikes the ground.

Playing into the wind can be confusing. One will think that because the wind is into you, you must swing harder to offset it. There are two problems with this thought/temptation; 1} the harder you swing, the less chance you have of striking the ball solidly, which will be a "dead duck" in the wind {Ha…a dead duck, I hope it's not a PuzzleDuck! :) had to do it} and 2} the harder you swing, the more spin you impart on the ball and the more it will tend to rise on you turning into a "flare".
Playing a smooth knockdown/three quarter shot with one extra club {ex. a 7 iron instead of an 8, depends on how strong the wind is; could be more of a drop in club} is again how I recommend playing into the wind. The knockdown will encourage solid contact and keep the ball low, and the smooth will impart less spin so it will penetrate more. When playing into the wind, it will be your friend in that it will help you control your ball when it strikes the ground.
If playing from the teeing area and, simply tee your ball lower. I have always been a fan of teeing lower and risking thin shots way before being one of floaters and flairs that were teed too high.
There is no need to try to "over power" the wind by over swinging. Play smarter, swing smoother and keep it down making solid contact and the wind will not affect your ball as much as you think. It can be your friend.

Knockdown

To knock a shot down, the shaft of the club must be leaning to the target. To do this you must get your weight to your forward leg, but in the correct sequence by pushing your right hip through the ball and not trying to hit "down" on the ball with your arms and shoulders. Always remember through. Refer to the Drills Chapter under Knockdown for pictures.

- Set up normally, except for slightly gripping down the grip and playing the ball slightly back in your stance. Choose one extra club {ex. a 7 iron instead of an 8}.

- Turn back against your braced right leg with a slightly shorter than normal backswing, but do not rush back to the ball. Give sequence a chance to develop. Remember, we are not trying to overpower the wind with effort, but to get into position to strike the ball solid and low. Again, to do this and get the shaft lean we need, we must push into the left and get your right side through the ball.

- Hold off your finish position to no more than shoulder height. This will encourage you to get into a solid impact position.

Dealing with trees

When in tree trouble, always take a moment and look at all of the possibilities {Fig. 19 – 5}. Look up as well as down {Fig. 19 – 6}. There are times when it is easier to get back into play by going over or through a gap to eliminate rough, bunkers, a hazard, getting you into position to have an easy pitch to the hole or even to play directly to the hole. Don't always look straight to the hole and think you have to go directly to it. Manage your game and play the percentages. Simply keep your options and mind open to all possibilities.

Fig. 19 – 5   Fig. 19 - 6

If you choose to play under the limbs {normally the safest way, but not always}, the first rule is to keep your ball under the limbs. Make sure to choose a club that will do so: error on the side of too low {Fig. 19 - 7}. If a ball gets up into limbs, it can go anywhere. This is again a great place for your "knockdown" shot, but do just that, keep it down and make sure to use a steep enough club.

Fig. 19 - 7

When laying up...lay up

There are times when we need to just eat our pride and "lay up" to a hazard or to a better position to attack the pin. When you choose to play wisely and do this, make sure that you do just that; keep the ball short of the hazard {Fig. 19 – 8}, or left or right {Fig. 19 – 9}. Error on the side of too much safe before trying to cozy up to the hazard to hit one club less in {Fig. 19 – 8a and 9a – great shot, but risky}. Missing a two foot putt doesn't chap you any more than "laying up" in the hazard!

Fig. 19 – 8   Fig. 19 – 8a

Fig. 19 – 9   Fig. 19 – 9a

Bending ball flight

I teach to hit straight shots so that bending a ball left or right is easier to do, see, and control. If you get to this level, you can really challenge the architect and the pin setter. It takes practice to control the correct amount, but it is fairly simple to bend the ball in either direction, especially if you normally play straight shots.

Setup is key:

Your grip should not change, but its' relationship to the clubface does {normal grip and face relationship Fig. 19 – 10}. The clubface should be closed relative to your normal grip the amount you want to bend the ball flight to the left {Fig. 19 – 11} and open relative to your normal grip the amount you wish to bend the ball to the right {Fig. 19 – 12}.

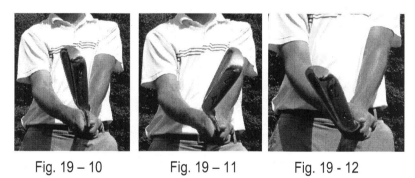

| Fig. 19 – 10 | Fig. 19 – 11 | Fig. 19 - 12 |

Aim the clubface at the target
Set your body lines {feet, arms, shoulders} the amount right of your target you wish the ball to bend to the left {Fig.19–13} or the amount left of your target you wish the ball to bend to the right   {Fig. 19 – 14}.

Fig. 19 - 13

Fig. 19 - 14

Fig. 19 – 15

Fig. 19 – 16

Fig. 19 - 17

Your ball position will appear back when bending to the left {Fig. 19 – 15} and forward when bending to the right {Fig. 19 – 16}, but should remain normal relative to your body lines.

Be sure to focus on where the ball must start rather than looking directly to the hole or your target {Fig. 19 – 17}. See the curve.

Swing

Make your normal swing. For bending the ball to the left, your arms should be soft and freely rotating {Fig. 19 – 18}. For bending the ball to the right, firm up your grip a touch to help you slightly hold off your release {Fig. 19 – 19}.

Fig. 19 – 18

Fig. 19 - 19

When you are trying to bend the ball flight, see it that way, think it that way, and feel it that way. You must mechanically do what is necessary to make it do so, but seeing, thinking, and feeling will help this ability quite a bit. See the curve/bend in your mind and feel it in your bones.

Flop

The last shot you should choose around the green, yet exciting and sometimes fun. The flop is a very dangerous shot to choose. It is a risk reward shot that will vary with your skill level. Even for the best players in the world, a miss is a big miss. Try to avoid them, but sometimes you just straight up need it…..so here you go.

The first thing we need is at least a relatively good lie {Fig. 19 – 20} so you can get the front edge of your club under the ball. The tighter the lie, the more dangerous this shot becomes {Fig. 19 – 20a}.

Fig. 19 – 20   Fig. 19 – 20a

The less bounce you have in your sand or "lob" wedge the easier this shot is. The next thing you need is speed. The more speed you have the higher you can flop it and, oh, by the way, the bigger your misses become. So, you need basically a full golf swing to hit a ball less than 30 yards.

Set up

- Your grip will remain the same, but its' relationship to the face will have the face slightly open {Fig. 19 – 21}.

- Put the ball slightly forward in a slightly wider stance {Fig. 19 – 21}.

- Aim the clubface at or slightly right of your target to open it and to compensate some for swinging across the ball. Aim your body lines to the left relative to how high you want to flop your ball {Fig. 19 – 21a}. More left means more open face, with more speed, which means more danger :). Be sure to keep your weight centered rather than let it creep to your back foot in an effort to "help" the ball up. There is also a tendency to do this the more open your stance is. Just be aware.

- Lean the shaft away from the target and point it to your center {Fig. 19 – 21}.

- Make a big ole swing and hold the face open through impact {Fig. 22 – 22, 22a and 23, 23a}.

Fig. 19 – 21   Fig. 19 – 22   Fig. 19 – 23

Fig. 19 – 21a   Fig. 19 – 22a   Fig. 19 – 23a

Things to be aware of:

- You must swing through the ball, not up and at it trying to help it up. The loft of the club will make the ball go up if you go through.
- Make sure your ball position is so that the bottom of your swing is at the ball. Make a few practice swings to see that spot.
- Stay centered and steady. Your weight will move very little in your backswing and through to your left in your through swing.

Ball in a divot or sitting down

If you play the game as it should be played, this will happen on occasions. This will be more difficult for the higher handicapper than the better player, because the better player strikes the ball first, regardless of the lie. To help do this, refer to the trusty.......you got it.......knock down shot. You may want to use one club less for this situation (an 8 iron instead of a 7). See the Drills Chapter and this one for how to play a knock down.

Rough

Depending on the season you are in and the climate, the rough at the course you are playing may vary in the type of grass and length. When in lighter rough it is not uncommon to get an anomaly called a "flyer", a "jumper", or a four letter word if you get one and it costs you strokes. A flyer is a ball that "jumps" off the face with less spin than normal because of the grass that gets between the ball and the club face, but is not thick enough to slow down your club {Fig. 19 – 24}. This will make the ball go further than normal in flight and in total distance because of that lack of spin, which makes distance control very difficult. Try to be aware of that possibility and club down properly. There is no science to guessing that correctly, but you can prepare to a degree by taking one club less when in light rough.

Fig. 19 - 24

When in deeper rough, it is first and foremost important to get the ball back into play and make sure that your next shot is from the fairway with an easy approach to the pin. The thicker rough will slow your club down and take away ball spin, so you will not be able to carry it as far and it will run more when it lands. If you cannot realistically get to the green make sure you do not have the same kind of shot out of thick rough again on your next. Play strategically to a higher percentage shot and get it up and down.

For deeper rough:

- Grip a little firmer. The taller and/or thicker rough will tend to grab the hozel of your club and flip the face closed. The firmer grip will help you hold it square.
- Play the ball slightly back in your stance so you will be striking a little more down on the ball and give less grass a chance to influence your swing speed and contact with the ball.
- Take a more lofted club if you can to help you cut through the grass. Sometimes you can move the ball further with less loft.
- Don't be shy, commit and as Stuart Maiden once said to Bobby Jones as a kid, "hit the Hell out of it".

Dress properly

This is obviously not a shot, but is actually more important and is not practiced regularly by most. Unless you are a Navy Seal, Army Special Forces, or Marine you will not do your best if you are not comfortable. This means that when you get wet, cold, hot, or are just miserable, you are most likely not going to focus on the things that need attention, but on how cold, wet, or hot you are. So, if performing your best is important, make sure to invest in a QUALITY rain suit, some under clothes that are thin and flexible yet warm for winter, and some clothing that keeps you cool in the summer. Always have a good water proof pair of shoes and hat to keep your feet and head dry {huge deal}, a hat for the summer in the sun, and a toboggan in the winter.

When you are comfortable you are much more apt to focus on the things that need your focus; like your game. Be prepared, have the correct mind set, and in inclement weather you will only have to be better than 25% of the field; the other 75% will give up.

Summary

20

There is so much you want to say and get down in a book, that it seems like there is never an end. We learn every day and hopefully get better EVERY day, so there is no end, just like the simple symbol that I use with my children to express to them how much I love them; a circle, there is no end { O }. I have been reading over and writing this book for years and there always seems to be a better way to say something or something that I have forgotten. There is always more to express, but it is what it is now. To summarize the PuzzleDuck Golf book;

- Smile!
- Have FUN! Do your best on EVERY shot, but don't take it so seriously. File the good ones and delete the bad ones. Enjoy the journey, being outside, nature, and being with friends; both old and new.
- Promote the game! It's the GREATEST of all time! :)
- Play by the rules. That means "as it lies" as well.
- Play with respect, honor, integrity, and manners.
- Respect and take care of the course.
- Respect your playing partners and opponents.
- Respect yourself.
- Give changes time......commit to a teacher/concept and give it time.
- Be a PuzzleDuck :)   Put the pieces together and migrate
- Be patiently impatient with the process.

- You can change in an "instant" if you tell yourself to. Believe and focus on that change, not the ball. The result is a product of the process.
- Get set up for success.
- Turn your left shoulder as far as your flexibility will allow behind the ball, to your right foot, and against your braced right leg.
- Keep it simple. Load, push, release. Compactly turn and coil against a braced back leg, push with that back leg and hip to the target {move the club with your right hip}, and time the face rotation from your shortest full swing to your longest. Putting and ChiPitching are obviously a little different by having a softer release. Putting uses only shoulders and back; but like your full swing, move the club through the ball with your right hip, knee, and foot in ChiPitching.
- Get that right side thru the ball in the proper sequence…..if it is……your ball can NOT go left and will go straighter and further. This means your weight and right hip not your shoulders. Yes, your right side as a whole "hits", but your shoulders and arms do not lead.
- Use the coordination, power, and feel of your dominant side .
- 1 back……..2 thru…….hold your finish position…..count to three……from your putter to your driver.
- Swing in balance and rhythm.
- Slow down……………
- Develop a Pre Shot Routine and stick with it on every shot you hit.
- Commit to every shot you chose to play….right or wrong and then evaluate the outcome.
- Swing relative to your flex ability….shorter is better than longer if that longer is broken down.

- Understand path and release. Your ball starts in the direction you swing and finishes where the clubface tells it to.

- Until you improve your path, match the release of your clubface to the path you tend to swing on.

- Hit the least lofted club the shot will allow around the greens

- Less wrist set/cock is more consistent than more. Let the loft of the club do the work. The longer your swing the more "natural" wrist set there will be. That wrist set is "flat", not cupped or bowed.

- Almost always think "THRU" the ball and not "DOWN" or "AT" the ball.

- Use your eyes correctly and look in curves on shots with break and when trying to curve a ball.

- Practice with a purpose and a direction. Migrate; remember there is no magic potion.

- Practice new swing adjustments without balls and slowly. This puts your focus on the adjustment.

- Play with a purpose. Be ready when it is your turn and get it done. Move with purpose.

- When playing through a group....remember....there is a reason they are letting you through.....THEY were slower.....take your NORMAL time......NO rush......many a round has been spoiled by rushing.

- Track your game and focus where you are the weakest and lose the most shots. Balance.

- Adapt and overcome.

- Stay positive and spread positive energy. Energy is contagious......make it good energy.

- Help someone, cause you "want" to not cause you "have" to.

- Do what you love and have passion for. There are different ways to measure wealth.
- Be who YOU are and enjoy EVERY minute given here! We are guaranteed NOTHING! Work hard, play hard, LIVE strong with honor and integrity. Sometimes you have to stand for what you believe in and know in your heart is right.....even if it hurts and you are standing alone. Cherish those that you love and that love you! I will take with me many SIMPLE experiences and memories money will NEVER be able to buy. Thank you for making it this far reading this book. It is my sincerest hope that it has been a positive experience for you in some way. PEACE.............until you have NO choice but to fight.........then finish the job.